T0305914

"Populism is the big topic in political science now. The study of the latest re-emergence of populist parties and leaders has managed to attract some of the most talented young scholars. In this rigorously researched book Petar Stankov offers an original theory of populist cycles, focusing on identity, economy and societal fairness. In addition, he offers empirical explanations of those cycles and valuable insights into the consequences of populist governance."

Ivan Krastev, Centre for Liberal Strategies, Sofia, Bulgaria, and Institute for Human Sciences, Vienna, Austria

"Petar Stankov's *The Political Economy of Populism* offers a clear and concise interpretation of how and why populist leaders and parties have emerged across many societies in recent decades. The book examines the consequences of the rise of populism, describing policies and results that typically follow populist ascendancies. Finally, the book explores self-correction mechanisms in mature democracies. Covering a wide range of cases and methods of analysis, the lucid prose and clear explanations will make this a 'must read' for every student of our current political moment."

Michael Kevane, Department of Economics, Santa Clara University, USA

"Despite the growing academic interest in populism, there is not much research about its relationship with the economy. This book addresses this research gap by offering a detailed analysis of the economic consequences of populism as well as a novel theory of populist cycles. This is a must read for all those who want to understand the economic underpinnings of populism."

Cristóbal Rovira Kaltwasser, School of Political Science, Diego Portales University, Santiago, Chile

The Political Economy of Populism

The Political Economy of Populism explores the interplay between identity, the economy and inequality to explain the dynamics of populist votes since the beginning of the 20th century.

The book discusses the political and economic implications of populist governance using data on populist incumbencies and linking it to historical data on the macro economy and democracy. Chapters draw from the most recent political science, economics and other social science literature, as well as historical data, to explain the long-term causes and consequences of populism. Populism emerges and gains traction when political entrepreneurs exploit underlying identity conflicts for political gains. As the distributional consequences of both economic distress and economic growth typically favor the elite over the poor and the lower middle class, economic shocks usually sharpen the underlying identity conflicts between the groups. The book provides evidence of significant differences in the ways fiscal and monetary policies are conducted by incumbent populists in Latin America, Europe and the OECD. The work concludes by suggesting avenues through which a 21st century social consensus can be built, so that our society can avoid repeating the mistakes that led to wars and failed economic experiments in the 20th century.

The Political Economy of Populism marks a significant contribution to the study of populism and is suited to students and scholars across the social sciences, including economics, political science and sociology.

Petar Stankov is a teaching fellow in the Department of Economics at Royal Holloway, University of London, UK, and a senior lecturer at the University of National and World Economy, Sofia, Bulgaria.

Routledge Frontiers of Political Economy

The Political Economy of Populism

An Introduction

Petar Stankov

Routledge
Taylor & Francis Group
LONDON AND NEW YORK

First published 2021
by Routledge
2 Park Square, Milton Park, Abingdon, Oxon OX14 4RN

and by Routledge
52 Vanderbilt Avenue, New York, NY 10017

Routledge is an imprint of the Taylor & Francis Group, an informa business

© 2021 Petar Stankov

The right of Petar Stankov to be identified as author of this work has been asserted by him in accordance with sections 77 and 78 of the Copyright, Designs and Patents Act 1988.

The Open Access version of this book, available at www.taylorfrancis .com, has been made available under a Creative Commons Attribution-Non Commercial-No Derivatives 4.0 license.

Trademark notice: Product or corporate names may be trademarks or registered trademarks, and are used only for identification and explanation without intent to infringe.

British Library Cataloguing-in-Publication Data
A catalogue record for this book is available from the British Library

Library of Congress Cataloging-in-Publication Data
A catalog record has been requested for this book

ISBN: 978-0-367-36802-9 (hbk)
ISBN: 978-0-429-35569-1 (ebk)

Typeset in Times New Roman
by Deanta Global Publishing Services, Chennai, India

To Gergana Stankova and Boris Stankov

Contents

Figures

Tables

About the Author

Petar Stankov is a teaching fellow in the Department of Economics at Royal Holloway, University of London, UK, and a senior lecturer at the University of National and World Economy, Sofia, Bulgaria. He has published on the political economy of populism, economic growth and liberalization and the variety of reform outcomes across countries. He earned a Ph.D. in Economics from CERGE-EI in Prague, the Czech Republic. He has taught undergraduate courses on the Economics of the European Union, Institutional Economics, Monetary Economics and Economic Growth, and postgraduate courses in Research Methodology and Evaluation Economics, among others.

Acknowledgments

I thank *Routledge* for their exceptional professionalism in dealing with the proposal, the first draft and the revised versions of this book. I would like to express my deep gratitude to the two anonymous referees whose critical comments contributed to the improvement of the first draft.

I also thank the Economics Departments at the University of National and World Economy (UNWE) in Sofia, Bulgaria and especially at Royal Holloway, University of London, for providing me natural teaching and research habitats. This work has greatly benefited from conversations with colleagues at both places.

A big thanks goes to Deborah Novakova (CERGE-EI) who helped edit the first draft. I am also eternally indebted to the *CERGE-EI Foundation* for long-term intellectual and financial support through its Graduate Teaching Fellowship and Career Integration Fellowship programs. Naturally, all errors and omissions are mine.

Finally, thanks—again—to Geri Stankova for putting up with the rest. You keep rocking, girl.

Thank you all.
Petar
December, 2019
Egham, UK

1 What do we know about populism?

Politics has polarized people with economic, social, and identity issues at least since the mid-19th century. Wars and deep economic crises have typically been associated with rising polarization. For example, after the relatively consensual pre-crisis decades, the Global Financial Crisis has reinvigorated politics and has unveiled broadening voter polarization in a growing number of countries. Over time, radical political preferences emerge, gain traction, receive representation, occasionally rise to the mainstream, and gradually die out in what appear to be recurring cycles (Edwards, 2019). This book explores the reasons these radical, populist cycles occur, and the interplay of their underlying factors.

The ascent of populism since the 1980s, and especially its post-crisis take-off, motivated this book. The surge of political extremes has received widespread attention from academics, media, and the general public. Published research has caught up with the public interest. Theoretical and empirical work on prominent aspects of populism – its drivers, modes of operation, and consequences – have earned well-deserved recognition. Recent work in various fields has advanced the explanations for populism on both ends of the political spectrum. Those fields include political science and sociology, and more recently, economics and economic history. However, we still lack a more general theory of cycles of populism, an empirical explanation of those cycles, and an overview of the more recent evidence of the political and economic consequences of populist governance. This book offers all three.

Recent political science literature has made significant progress in uncovering the defining characteristics of populism. Müller (2016) states the necessary and sufficient conditions for a politician to be considered a populist: the necessary condition is an anti-elitist election platform, and the sufficient condition is anti-pluralism. According to the same author, a defining feature of populism is its polarizing effect on the electorate, as it thrives on conflict between two groups with antagonistic identities: *the people* and *the elite*. Throughout this book, identity is understood as one's perception of self along multiple dimensions.

The identity conflict behind populism is well described by Mudde and Rovira Kaltwasser (2017, pp. 5–6). Based on a number of case studies of right-wing European parties, left-wing presidents in Latin America, and the Tea Party movement in the United States, they believe that populism is an ideology that divides societies into antagonistic camps. Drawing upon earlier research (Stanley, 2008), they accept that populism is a "thin" ideology, which borrows features of other classic ideologies to appease *the people* and denounce *the elite*.

The "thinness" of the populist quasi-ideology is now a dominant feature of the way political scientists define it (Bonikowski et al., 2019). However, because populism draws from a variety of ideologies, its precise definition has always been, and perhaps will always be, elusive. In turn, the lack of a common ideological origin of populists has resulted in a multitude of ways to approach the phenomenon (Gidron and Bonikowski, 2013). Political scientists approach it as confrontational communication evolving around local ideological or identity issues, irrespective of whether the leader, the party, or the ideology is currently dominant or not. In contrast, economists typically see populism as a narrower set of policies of the *incumbent* politicians, who ignore the economic risks associated with those policies, predominantly for political gain (Acemoglu, 2013; Dornbusch and Edwards, 1990).

Both approaches capture important aspects of populism. Until very recently, however, a unified framework had not been developed. This may be about to change with the work by Besley and Persson (2019). They effectively blend the two fields in a model of dynamic individual identity formation, and evolving voter and incumbent party preferences, which allows for endogenous emergence of competition to incumbent parties from the political fringe. The equilibrium policies in their model become a function of "political conflicts between traditional political elites, who control established parties formed around economic interests, and an evolving share of citizens who unite on a non-economic dimension of politics" (Besley and Persson, 2019, p. 3). Thus, widening divisions between *the elite* and *the people* exhibit cyclical behavior, which has thus far evaded explanation. In equilibrium, this cyclical behavior depends on two parameters: the importance voters place on identity issues, and income polarization.

Currently, authoritarian populism, typically based on identity politics, is more relevant in Europe, the USA, and some parts of Asia and Africa, while redistributional populism prevails in Latin America. The distinction between the two brands of populism, however, has not always been sharply drawn, and, indeed, has displayed cyclical behavior. Mudde and Rovira Kaltwasser (2011) argue that European and Latin American brands of populism are not different *per se*. Rather, their differences stem from the ideologies they adopt to generate broad appeal of their divisive platforms to *the people* – who collectively constitute a key player in the political platforms of populists. The ideologies adopted may be socialism, liberalism, or nationalism, differing in each national context. At the same time, populism lacks key common elements: a *common* history, electoral base, international coordination, key texts laying out its intellectual foundations, iconic leaders of international acclaim, or a calendar of its significant moments in history, all of which are typical in other traditional ideologies (Canovan, 2004; Mudde and Rovira Kaltwasser, 2013).

The lack of common key elements is the main reason we cannot think of populism as a stand-alone ideology. We can define it as a quasi-ideology, or better still, **a political strategy, which creates and nurtures radically conflicting identities for political gain**. Exploiting these gains, however, is not always possible, as Chapter 2 will illustrate. It will become clear that political payoffs depend on the interplay between the state of the economy and the state of the identity of the target voters. In turn, the joint impact of those economic and identity factors will be determined by the current social and demographic characteristics, including inequality of opportunity and income, and the education, skills, and age of the target voters.

The next chapter offers insights into how these interact to produce long-term populist cycles. This necessarily implies that before they begin to explore the potential political gains, political entrepreneurs need to create a conflict of identities in the first place. This is a process described by Laclau (2005) in the context of constructing the notion of *the people*. The conflict between identities is a feature of *political creative destruction*, in which potential entrants into the political mainstream innovate with various electoral tools to broaden their appeal and to oust incumbent politicians.

There is more than a broad appeal involved in the rise of populism. Motivated by recent electoral trends towards populist parties and emerging scholarship, Abromeit (2017) reviews advances in political science literature. In this literature, there are currently four dominant approaches to studying populism:

1. *The discourse-historical approach*, represented by Wodak (2015). On the one hand, a pivotal element of right-wing populism is its rhetorical strategies. These are centered around nationalism, anti-otherness (-Semitism, -Islam, -immigrants), political performance, and gender roles. On the other hand, according to the approach, populism has no single explanation. Therefore, one needs to zoom in on the local historical context around turning points of voter mobilization to explain it.

2. The political performance approach, which defines populism as *a political communication style*, is a trademark of both left- and right-wing populism. Both left- and right-wing populists employ certain performance strategies (Moffitt, 2016; Rode and Revuelta, 2015). This communication style is independent of the ideology – the focus is on how the message is delivered rather than on its underlying content.

3. *The "ideational" approach to populism.* In essence, populism is a set of ideas (Mudde and Rovira Kaltwasser, 2017, p. 62). They consist of a certain view of the world being attached to a well-established ideology, e.g. socialism or liberalism, and a few key recurring concepts: *the people, the elite*, and the general *will of the people* (Mudde and Rovira Kaltwasser, 2013). Abromeit (2017, p. 181) argues that Mudde and Rovira Kaltwasser (2017) provide a "good overview of the transformation of populism in the U.S. over the course of the twentieth century from a predominantly progressive, to a predominantly reactionary movement." To understand this shift, however, Abromeit et al. (2015) call for a more comprehensive and interdisciplinary method than that offered by the ideational approach, a method which would be able to explain the inherent defects of democracy.

4. *The defective democracy approach*, discussed by Müller (2016), centers around the legitimacy of elected politicians. The legitimacy of the current elite is undermined using purely political methods to reduce democracy to a spectacle via showmanship. This argument is fully developed by Müller (2016). The legitimacy of a democracy can be undermined for economic reasons as well. Just as democracy was consolidated in Western Europe when the social welfare state gained traction in the 1950s and 1960s, the Global Financial Crisis (GFC) undermined the legitimacy of mainstream parties. Due to their relative consensus on how economic policies should be conducted prior to the GFC, the establishment parties differed from each other only narrowly. At the same time, their representatives were considered to belong to the elite. The GFC served as a trigger for deeply rooted societal discontent, which demanded new political representation. This essentially economic explanation for the loss of the political legitimacy of mainstream parties is explored in a narrative by Judis (2016) and in an empirical work by Stankov (2018), among others.

Abromeit et al. (2015) and Abromeit (2017) argue that the best approach to explaining populism is rooted in a general social theory developed between the 1920s and the 1970s at the Institute for Social Research at the University of Frankfurt, Germany (the Frankfurt School). The part of this theory which is relevant to populism tackles the mechanisms of emergence and consolidation of inherently anti-democratic ideologies within a democratic system.

This is possible, the Frankfurt School argues – notably in Adorno et al. (1950) – if the democratic system, while formally guaranteeing certain rights for everyone, is functionally unable to deliver on its promise of economic progress for the masses.

Indeed, as Chapter 3 illustrates, extreme political preferences were essentially marginalized as the social welfare state was gradually rolled out across Europe after World War II. However, today, they are resurgent. Why is populism re-emerging now in the same democracies which have achieved the most generous "cradle-to-grave" social welfare systems humanity has ever seen? Why is populism also surging now in the new democracies in Central and Eastern Europe (CEE), where the people have never lived better than now? Why did it not emerge and flourish in the early 1990s when the entire CEE region was undergoing a socially ruinous transformation recession on par with, if not worse than, the Great Depression (World Bank, 2002, p. 5)? Perhaps we need a new interdisciplinary theory of populism to answer these questions. The cultural backlash hypothesis (Norris and Inglehart, 2019) offers new insights into salient identity-based features of the radical vote but, alas, places secondary importance on its economic drivers. The analysis in the next chapter presents one possible avenue for development of such a theory, in which identity issues and socio-economic shocks play key *combined* roles.

The analysis above implies that there is a need for **three important innovations in the study of populism**. First, we need an interdisciplinary treatment of populism which combines elements of contemporary political science, economics, and sociology to illustrate populism's triggers and dynamic drivers. Second, we also need a rigorous empirical approach to identify how the elements of the theory connect with observable electoral outcomes at the extreme ends of the political spectrum. Third, understanding why populism is on the rise now demands that we examine its longer-term cyclicality.

An interdisciplinary theory of populism is needed mainly for two reasons. First, as we have seen, the various traits of populism have been best identified in the political science literature. With its multiple approaches, political science literature reaches great depth in explaining populist dynamics. Yet, apart from some notable exceptions, e.g. Eguia and Giovannoni (2019), it lacks a certain degree of the rigorousness typical in other social sciences.

The rigor is not needed for its own sake, but because understanding contemporary populism necessarily requires an explanation of longer-term populist cycles intensifying *within* a rich liberal democracy. An explanation could be best delivered with some formalization capturing the characteristics of the current developed economies. Chapter 2 reviews the contributions of political science and economics which help address endogenously emerging populism.

The promising new approaches to understanding the dynamics of populism model extreme votes – the votes for extremist political candidates and platforms – as political equilibrium phenomena in identity-motivated socio-economic markets for policies. Virtually all contribute to the seminal work by Akerlof and Kranton (2000), who brought identity issues into mainstream economics, after notable earlier efforts by Kevane (1997), among others. The most recent directions in the field are offered by Besley and Persson (2019), Collier (2019), and Shayo (2020), who think of identity as a dynamic phenomenon which interacts with economic factors to affect equilibrium voter preferences.

Second, until very recently, rigorous studies of populism by economists have ignored the fact that voters view themselves as parts of larger groups. This sense of belonging to a certain group, which is typically recognized in sociology studies, is important to incorporate into economic models because the economic fortunes of those groups can alter individual voter behavior in politically relevant ways. This is because those groups may be on the winning or the losing distributional end of an economic reform, e.g. trade, financial, or labor market liberalization.

The literature has successfully offered methods to link voter behavior, not only to their own prosperity, but also to the fortunes of a reference group they associate themselves with. Then, the interdisciplinary approach to politically relevant individual behavior can be modeled by extending political economy models with elements from social identity theory. This is precisely the approach Grossman and Helpman (2018) and Shayo (2020) take in a promising new direction in the political economy of reforms.

From an empirical standpoint, there have been three dominant methods of studying populism. A rising number of studies explain populism directly by looking at the patterns of voting behavior for predefined populist parties across Europe and Latin America and relating those voting patterns to a set of economic shocks (Algan et al., 2017; Fetzer, 2019; Stankov, 2018). Other studies look at specific electoral events – e.g. the Brexit referendum or a US election cycle – and use within-country variation of voter responses to trade, financial, and migration shocks to capture the drivers of populist demand (Autor, Dorn, Hanson, and Majlesi, 2016; Autor, Dorn, and Hanson, 2016; Becker et al., 2017; Jensen et al., 2017). A more traditional line of literature still looks at case studies of a limited number of similar countries (Toplišek, 2020). The case studies predominantly use descriptive methods to go deeper than most into the local contextual explanations of populist votes. Although this approach yields valuable information to supplement larger-scale studies, its overview of the more general trends is rather limited.

The following chapters discuss three systemic shocks which underpin the extreme vote cycles: shocks to identity, economic shocks, and fairness shocks. It is not trivial to disentangle which shock triggers others in a given context. It is probably a safe assumption that larger shocks in one domain will likely trigger tremors in others, thereby amplifying the impact of each individual shock on extreme votes. Identity shocks are driven by migration and inequality dynamics; economic shocks arise from recessions, austerity, and broader globalization trends, such as trade and financial openness; and fairness shocks are determined by how voters perceive substantive and procedural fairness in a given society. The impact of these shocks on the shape of the populist vote is discussed in Chapter 2.

Bibliography

Abromeit, J. (2017). A critical review of recent literature on populism. *Politics and Governance*, *5*(4), 177–186.

Abromeit, J., Norman, Y., Marotta, G., & Chesterton, B. (2015). *Transformations of populism in Europe and the Americas: History and recent tendencies*. Bloomsbury Publishing.

Acemoglu, D., Egorov, G., & Sonin, K. (2013). A political theory of populism. *The Quarterly Journal of Economics*, *128*(2), 771–805.

Adorno, T., Frenkel-Brunswik, E., Levinson, D., & Sanford, R. (1950). *The authoritarian personality*. Harper & Row, Inc.

Akerlof, G. A., & Kranton, R. E. (2000). Economics and identity. *The Quarterly Journal of Economics*, *115*(3), 715–753.

Algan, Y., Guriev, S., Papaioannou, E., & Passari, E. (2017). The European trust crisis and the rise of populism. *Brookings Papers on Economic Activity*, 309–383.

Autor, D., Dorn, D., Hanson, G., & Majlesi, K. (2016). Importing political polarization? The electoral consequences of rising trade exposure. Working Paper 22637, National Bureau of Economic Research.

Autor, D. H., Dorn, D., & Hanson, G. H. (2016). The China shock: Learning from labor-market adjustment to large changes in trade. *Annual Review of Economics*, *8*(1), 205–240.

Becker, S. O., Fetzer, T., & Novy, D. (2017). Who voted for Brexit? A comprehensive district-level analysis. *Economic Policy*, *32*(92), 601–650.

Besley, T., & Persson, T. (2019). The rise of identity politics. Working Paper, London School of Economics.

Bonikowski, B., Halikiopoulou, D., Kaufmann, E., & Rooduijn, M. (2019). Populism and nationalism in a comparative perspective: A scholarly exchange. *Nations and Nationalism*, *25*(1), 58–81.

Canovan, M. (2004). Populism for political theorists? *Journal of Political Ideologies*, *9*(3), 241–252.

Collier, P. (2019). Diverging identities: A model of class formation. Working Paper SM-WP-2019–01, Blavatnik School of Government, University of Oxford.

Dornbusch, R., & Edwards, S. (1990). Macroeconomic populism. *Journal of Development Economics*, *32*(2), 247–277.

Edwards, S. (2019). On Latin American populism, and its echoes around the world. *Journal of Economic Perspectives*, *33*(4), 76–99.

Eguia, J. X., & Giovannoni, F. (2019). Tactical extremism. *American Political Science Review*, *113*(1), 282–286.

Fetzer, T. (2019). Did austerity cause Brexit? *American Economic Review*, *109*(11), 3849–3886.

Gidron, N., & Bonikowski, B. (2013). Varieties of populism: Literature review and research agenda. Technical Report 13-0004, Weatherhead Center.

Grossman, G. M., & Helpman, E. (2018). Identity politics and trade policy. Working Paper 25348, National Bureau of Economic Research.

Jensen, J. B., Quinn, D. P., & Weymouth, S. (2017). Winners and losers in international trade: The effects on U.S. presidential voting. *International Organization*, *71*(03), 423–457.

Judis, J. B. (2016). *The populist explosion: How the great recession transformed American and European politics*. Columbia University Press.

Kevane, M. (1997). Can there be an 'identity economics'? Working Paper, Santa Clara University.

Laclau, E. (2005). *On populist reason*. Phronesis Series. Verso.

Moffitt, B. (2016). *The global rise of populism: Performance, political style and representation*. Stanford University Press.

Mudde, C., & Rovira Kaltwasser, C. (2017). *Populism: A very short introduction*. Oxford University Press.

Mudde, C., & Rovira Kaltwasser, C. (2011). *Voices of the peoples: Populism in Europe and Latin America compared*. Technical Report, Kellog Institute for International Studies.

Mudde, C., & Rovira Kaltwasser, C. (2013). Populism. In M. Freeden & M. Stears (Eds.), *The Oxford handbook of political ideologies*. Oxford University Press.

Müller, J. (2016). *What is populism?* University of Pennsylvania Press.

Norris, P., & Inglehart, R. (2019). *Cultural backlash and the rise of populism: Trump, Brexit, and authoritarian populism*. Cambridge University Press.

Rode, M., & Revuelta, J. (2015). The wild bunch! An empirical note on populism and economic institutions. *Economics of Governance 16*(1), 73–96.

Shayo, M. (2020). Social identity and economic policy. *Annual Review of Economics 12*, forthcoming.

Stankov, P. (2018). The political economy of populism: An empirical investigation. *Comparative Economic Studies*, *60*(2), 230–253.

Stanley, B. (2008). The thin ideology of populism. *Journal of Political Ideologies*, *13*(1), 95–110.

Toplišek, A. (2020). The political economy of populist rule in post-crisis Europe: Hungary and Poland. *New Political Economy*, *25*(3), 388–403.

Wodak, R. (2015). *The politics of fear: What right-wing populist discourses mean*. Sage Publishing.

World Bank. (2002). *Transition, the first ten years: Analysis and lessons for Eastern Europe and the Former Soviet Union*. World Bank.

2 A theory of populist cycles

2.1 Why cycles?

Since the fall of the Berlin Wall in 1989, the number of democracies around the world has steadily increased (Center for Systemic Peace, 2019). However, the Global Financial Crisis (GFC) brought challenges to the political systems of almost every democracy, which the mainstream parties have been mostly ill-equipped to deal with. Those challenges originate in three interrelated socio-economic domains: identity, economy, and fairness. Turning points in democratization and authoritarianization occur when the interplay of these domains creates a large-scale demand for political change. The central argument in this chapter is that shocks in the three domains trigger demand-driven political change. The change is latent until political entrepreneurs match voter demands in political platforms addressing their concerns about identity, the economy, and fairness. If the shocks in those domains are deep and concurrent, the observed political change can be profound, similar to the one we observed in the aftermath of the GFC.

History is rich in examples of demand-driven cyclical political regime change. Acemoglu and Robinson (2001) lay out the cyclical behavior of political regimes by developing a model of class competition between the rich ruling elite and the disenfranchised poor. The model implicitly assumes that the identities of the two groups have already been formed, and are fixed – an assumption which we will relax below. The authors argue that during recessions, the opportunity costs of a revolution organized by the poor class are low; when they have already lost much of their income to the recession, they are likely to feel that they have little left to lose. In such contexts, a revolution in which the ruling elite is overthrown for economic reasons becomes more likely. There is plenty of evidence for increasingly likely regime change in times of economic distress (Geddes, 1999).

The reason the above theory is credible is that the state of the economy changes the nature of the existing identity conflicts between the rich and the poor, and may amplify or subdue them. Conflicts often become more pronounced during periods of rising income inequality (Pastor and Veronesi, 2018) and commodity price booms (Boucekkine et al., 2016; Ocampo, 2015), as well as during economic downturns (Algan et al., 2017).

With surging identity tensions, the elite faces an increasingly credible threat of a revolution – a regime change in which they lose most rents from their incumbency. To prevent a revolution, the elite may choose to give more political freedom to the poor, which is the essence of democratization. For example, democratization can lead to universal suffrage to reduce political tensions between the classes. This story fits the somewhat paradoxical notion that populism can enhance democracy, especially in an autocratic society. History has demonstrated that in some cases, most notably in Latin America, populism can be inclusive (Mudde and Rovira Kaltwasser, 2011) and "depending on its electoral power and the context in which it arises, populism can work as *either* a threat to *or* a corrective for democracy" (Mudde and Rovira Kaltwasser, 2017, p. 83).

If the elite enfranchises the poor because they find the threat of a revolution credible, then populism has seemingly served its corrective function: it has empowered the poor class and has restored *procedural* fairness in a given society. But what happens after a new or strengthened democracy has come about? Having established their political representation, the demands of the poor tend to increase. They demand not only political freedoms, but also economic redistribution to restore *substantive* fairness. As the majority of voters are poor and see themselves as different from the elite, they demand redistribution through taxation and transfers. Such policies can lead to radical redistribution and stifling of competitive markets, as in Latin America after World War II, or to more inclusive welfare states and integrated markets, as in post-WWII Western Europe.

As a redistribution policy stance typically correlates with fewer free markets, policies directed at limiting or ending globalization soon follow. Giordani and Mariani (2019, p. 1) explain the intuition:

> [G]lobalization breeds its own decline. Human capital accumulation is initially sustained by a high level of redistribution, which makes globalization politically viable. Eventually, however, the lack of support for redistribution brought about by the rise of the educated class favors the emergence of protectionist policies.

Thus, identity conflicts between the rich and the poor do not disappear, but they are founded on new grounds: substantive fairness. In essence, substantive fairness concerns arise when income and wealth inequality become increasingly salient issues to voters who have recently found political freedoms.

It takes a global economic crisis of the magnitude of the Great Depression or the GFC for the identity tensions between the rich and the poor to resurface. It is notable that within-country income inequality has been on the rise at least since the early 1980s (WID.World, 2019), but a vote surge for extreme parties only took off after the GFC. Thus, a large-scale economic crisis serves as a demand-side trigger for political activism to stem the rise of income of the rich: "The backlash is inevitable, just a matter of time. Globalization carries the seeds of its own destruction" (Pastor and Veronesi, 2018, p. 2). An economic crisis may bring other identity issues to the fore, which are not necessarily related to substantive fairness, e.g. a conflict between migrants and native workers, or racial tensions. The lines along which the identity conflict is modeled may be different, but the outcome is always the same: a growing demand for populist platforms on either end of the political spectrum.

If and when populists are elected, they design policies almost identically.

> Despite coming to power in different historical and cultural contexts, their approach is the same: they stack key political institutions with loyalists and allies [...] and muzzle the media through legislation and censorship. Their slow and piecemeal approach makes it difficult to pinpoint when the collapse of democracy actually happens.
>
> (Kendall-Taylor et al., 2019, p. 3)

Thus, most populists apply a textbook-like, paradigmatic approach to establishing their own authority, which leads to democratic erosion in the name of the very people who elected them.

The similarity of populist *modus operandi* across countries and time leads to a natural shift in how we approach the understanding of their regimes: "a large literature in political science [...] has argued that a major shift has been underway for some time shifting from traditional left-right spectrum towards greater importance of an authoritarian-liberalism dimension" (Besley and Persson, 2019, p. 37). Gidron and Bonikowski (2013) and Kendall-Taylor et al. (2019) provide further in-depth reviews of the political science literature on democratic erosion.

A culmination of the democratic erosion is a pure, fully articulated repressive authoritarian regime of the sort Mussolini, Hitler, and Stalin developed in 1920s and 1930s Italy, Germany, and the Soviet Union, and of the sort communist dictators adopted between the 1950s and 1980s in Central and Eastern Europe. However, this extreme is not necessarily the outcome, as today's facade democracies in Europe, Latin America, Africa, and Asia demonstrate.

Bértoa and Weber (2019) argue that economic crises may act as a trigger for further democratization in restrained democracies, but also that a consolidated democracy may never reach ultimate stability due to recurring crises. Hybrid regime states can remain – with a mix of democratic and authoritarian elements – in which leaders superficially embrace democratic institutions and the rule of law, but manipulate them to serve their own interests (Kendall-Taylor et al., 2019, p. 4).

Manipulation of local institutions is accompanied by a transformation of the leader's identity; once inseparable from *the people*, a populist leader is now an inherent part of the ruling elite. They oppress the same people who elected them through a democratic election, although they continue to articulate themselves as inseparable from the people. As Krastev (2017, p. 6) points out, "The question is no longer whether it's possible for Hitler to come back; it's whether we'd even be able to recognize him."

As portraying themselves as part of the people prolongs their political longevity, it is vital for populist authoritarian leaders to be able to control the political narrative through their grip on mass mainstream and targeted social media; even though their populist policies can be economically damaging and detrimental to democracy, they create a new identity-based belief system with its own rents, which voters internalize. Those rents come from having a well-articulated enemy of *the people*: the immigrants, the European Union, or "rotting capitalism." In any case, an identity conflict acts as a prerequisite to the creation of identity rents. In turn, the identity rents populist leaders create for their voters solve the compliance problem the leaders have on their hands due to the deteriorating state of the economy (Collier, 2019b).

As long as the identity rents exist, and as long as they outweigh the economic and political costs of an autocratic populist regime, the regime survives. However, the regime cannot survive forever, because it can neither sustain its identity rents indefinitely nor can it keep the voters from realizing the large economic and political costs of the regime indefinitely. Ultimately, *populism fatigue* emerges naturally (Stankov, 2017a), which leads to renewed demands for political change.

Escaping an authoritarian populist regime is feasible, but costly, and may require credible government commitment to a new regime, which means significant human capital investment for new generations and renewed trade liberalization (Blanchard and Willmann, 2011). Further, to avoid reform reversals and coups arising from conflicting intra-elite groups, the conflicting groups need to have a common policy liberalization platform (Galiani and Torrens, 2014). In addition, as Gros (2017) has shown, when the electorate forms their values and political opinions faster than the parties address them, the political system becomes inherently unstable. This is precisely the reason social networks have acted as a platform for democratization in restrained regimes, and as a platform for authoritarianization in consolidated democracies. To avoid instability, mainstream parties and leaders need to learn how to "feel the pulse" of the voters much faster. Ultimately, voters' pulse rate accelerates when issues related to their identity, the economy, and fairness arise. Sections 2.2, 2.3, and 2.4 illustrate how.

2.2 Identity

The term *identity politics* appeared in research work in the late 1970s, and by the 1990s had gradually been adopted by a number of social scientists, who explored differences across groups along a given dimension, be it social status, minority, nation, race, or ethnicity (Bernstein, 2005). Why and how does identity – one's feeling about one's self and one's own group – shape both economic outcomes and political preferences?

In a groundbreaking article, Akerlof and Kranton (2000) provide a convincing story. A person's identity affects decision-making. People care about what and how much they consume, and about their income. However, they also follow certain *identity prescriptions* – courses of action attached to the groups they identify with. Conforming to prescribed actions affirms a person's identity, thereby raising the value of what they are trying to achieve in life. In contrast, an identity deviation imposes certain tangible and intangible costs. As a result, Akerlof and Kranton (2000) argue, choosing one's identity changes the payoff structure of all decisions. In addition, their decisions can also feed back into their identity payoffs. The interplay between the identity and choices of any individual is further enriched by the fact that choices others make – i.e., the groups they associate with or any other third parties – also affect identity payoffs.

How is the interplay between identity and choices politically relevant? First, according to Akerlof and Kranton (2000), identity can explain behavior which is detrimental. On the one hand, people may cast votes for extreme candidates even when they realize that populist policies are economically harmful. Both classic and recent research suggests that populists' economic platforms generally ignore basic principles of good governance and economics (Dalio et al., 2017; Dornbusch and Edwards, 1990; Edwards, 2019). On the other hand, the harm done to voters by the execution of populist platforms is more than made up for by their feeling of restored identity. Consequently, once treated as inexplicable or arbitrary (Brennan and Buchanan, 1984), voter migration to the extreme now seems reasonable and well within the boundaries of public choice theory – a theory applying economic methods to the study of political processes beginning with the works of Downs (1957) and Riker and Ordeshook (1968). From a theoretical standpoint, seemingly erratic voter outcomes thus become well-behaved, especially when identity is thought to alter the structure of both costs and benefits of a given voter behavior.

Second, Akerlof and Kranton (2000) discuss how identity creates a new type of externality, which we may call an *outsider externality*. Once an outsider enters a group which has already adopted a well-established identity, the outsider imposes identity costs on the incumbents in the group. They feel threatened by the otherness among them. This is politically relevant, especially in the case of immigration. As migrants are different from the established members of a society in a variety of ways, they impose identity costs on the native part of that society. Those costs are rising with the number of immigrants a country admits. To restore their identity rents, some native voters turn to extreme parties, because parties in the center do not recognize the existence of identity costs. Thus, significant parts of the traditional center-left and center-right electorate feel misrepresented by politicians who still believe the key issue for voters is still the economy. It may still be for many, but increasingly, it isn't. When identity becomes more important than the economy, parties creating and nurturing identity conflicts gain. This process has been documented at the EU level by Schlueter et al. (2013) and, more recently, by Meuleman et al. (2019).

Third, Akerlof and Kranton (2000) contend that identity plays a direct role in shaping preferences for consumption. The argument lends itself to political preferences in a class of consumer behavior models called *extended preferences models*. Akerlof and Kranton (2000) conclude that identity-based preferences constitute a common framework for analysis of numerous social outcomes. It is also clearly applicable to extreme political preferences. In the extended preferences models, "preferences depend on arguments other than the standard consumption goods" (Romer, 1996, p. 201). In the politically relevant case, a voter's total satisfaction depends on satisfaction derived from both consumption and from the act of voting itself.

Although extending preferences with the utility of voting is a step forward in understanding *voting*, it is not particularly helpful in explaining *extreme* voting, once people have decided to vote. Efforts to combine economic and social factors to explain radical votes are long-standing in political science literature (Betz, 1993), but most contributions are at an intuitive level and lack formalization. Studying transitions of voter preferences to political extremes requires a richer modeling structure, which can be derived from a few key contributions.

Once the members of a certain group feel threatened by outsiders, they are not only willing to vote to harm themselves by electing populist parties with detrimental economic platforms, they are also willing to impose additional costs on outsiders, because their own identity has been undermined. Using the jargon of economics, spiteful (punitive) preferences of incumbents render punishment to the out-group optimal: a classic argument in the political economy of hatred (Glaeser, 2005). A harm done to the out-group creates an additional benefit to the in-group, which compensates them for their identity losses. In other words, by voting far-left or far-right, the insiders are willing to punish outsiders, even though the punishment can also harm the insiders.

The result above – that punishment of others may be politically optimal – is not only driving voters to the polls, it incentivizes them to vote for extreme parties, because extreme parties sell punitive slogans. Notice that the punitive drive to the extremes is not necessarily directed at a single group of outsiders. It can be channeled at *any* group of outsiders, so long as they impose identity costs on the insiders, and can push the voter to either the far-left or the far-right, depending on the type of identity costs imposed on the insiders.

For example, punishments can be channeled at immigrants by imposing greater costs on their arrival and stay in the country, and by voting for far-right parties supplying those punishments. Punishments can also be aimed at the "corrupt elite" via far-left redistribution platforms. And while it is optimal for voters to polarize in the presence of identity costs, it is also optimal for political entrepreneurs on the political fringes to "supply hate-creating stories to further their own objectives" (Glaeser, 2005, p. 47).

Despite the evidence that immigrants contribute more to advanced economies than they take out (Brown et al., 2019; Dustmann and Frattini, 2014), one of the most contentious issues in post-crisis election campaigns has been immigration. Why has immigration gained prominence in voter concerns? Apparently, it is not the actual economic impact of migrants that local voters worry about, but the fact that having immigrants around has some intangible effect on how voters *feel* about their own lives and their communities: "Worries about immigration have played a major role in the rise of extremist parties across Europe, the Brexit referendum, and Trump's presidential campaign," according to Poutvaara and Steinhardt (2018, p. 471). The rise of immigration is producing a significant boost for extreme votes in Austria (Halla et al., 2017), France (Edo et al., 2019; Jolly and DiGiusto, 2014), Italy (Caselli et al., 2019), Germany (Karapin, 1998), and Switzerland (Krishnakumar and Müller, 2012), among other developed countries. Evidence for 25 OECD economies between 1980 and 2008 suggests that a "greater influx of immigrants has led policy-makers to increase welfare state spending" (Gaston and Rajaguru, 2013, p. 90), in an effort to compensate more vulnerable workers for the identity costs imposed on them by immigration.

Voter polarization in the presence of identity costs requires the existence of identity costs in the first place. Political psychology work has shown that those costs are significant (Hainmueller and Hopkins, 2014). Who are the voters most likely to experience identity costs, and what are their character-istics? Among other factors, education and skills of local constituents have received considerable attention in both the empirical and the theoretical literature. For example, Mayda (2006) argues that – in addition to the non-economic factors forming attitudes towards migrants, virtually all of which affect identity costs – a key economic factor determining attitudes towards migration is the skill composition of natives relative to migrants in the des-tination country. She uses a Heckscher-Ohlin framework to show that if a country is endowed with more skilled natives, they will favor migration of less-skilled workers. However, if a country has a significant share of low-skilled workers, they will prefer high-skilled migration. Mayda (2006) uses individual-level data from the National Identity module of the International Social Survey Program (ISSP) to test her hypothesis for the demand side of the political market in 22 countries.

The hypothesis has been re-tested on the supply side by studying actual immigration policy votes in the US Congress from 1970 until 2006 (Facchini and Steinhardt, 2011), and on the demand side in Europe by Ortega and Polavieja (2012) and in the USA by Scheve and Slaughter (2001). Iturbe-Ormaetxe and Romero (2016, p. 159) also find a skills divide in political preferences towards immigration: "the higher the political weight of the rich (highly skilled) is, the less tolerant the poor and the middle-class are toward immigration and the more demanding they are toward increasing public spending."

The overarching message is nearly exactly the same: "representatives from more skilled labor abundant districts are more likely to support an open immigration policy towards the unskilled, whereas the opposite is true for representatives from more unskilled labor abundant districts" (Facchini and Steinhardt, 2011, p. 734). Education has also played a role in deter-mining the outcome of the Brexit referendum, with less-educated voters predominantly choosing to leave the EU (Alabrese et al., 2019; Becker et al., 2017).

Apart from the education levels of native voters, the predominant pat-terns of migrant education levels and skills are also politically relevant. Using data from 12 national elections in Europe between 2007 and 2016, Moriconi et al. (2018) found that high-skilled migration turns voters away from nationalistic parties, while low-skilled migration pivots them towards nationalism. Why? Within an identity-based preferences framework, the answer is obvious: the identity costs of high-skilled workers induced by immigration of any type do exist, but are lower than the economic benefits from immigration. Also, high-skilled workers think favorably of parties advancing free markets, including free labor markets. This is in line with the outcomes discussed by Karakas and Mitra (2019, p. 22), who argue that voter behavior may decouple from traditional dividing lines such as income, education, or economic ideologies. Instead, cultural identities may determine both voting and equilibrium policies of the incumbent parties: "cultural affiliation of the equilibrium policies need not agree with the cultural identity of the electorally-dominant group." This implies that high-skilled workers may vote for policy proposals favoring both high-skilled *and* low-skilled immigration.

The thought processes of the low-skilled voters are different. They do not feel a significant economic benefit from any type of immigration. They *feel* wage stagnation because of *stories* of migrants "taking" their jobs or undermining their wages. The evidence in favor of those stories is scarce, even when native workers and immigrants compete for the same jobs. Friedberg and Hunt (1995, p. 42) review evidence from the developed countries and find that "a 10 percent increase in the fraction of immigrants in the population reduces native wages by at most 1 percent." More recent evidence also fails to find a significant reduction in wages as a result of immigration (Hainmueller et al., 2015).

The neutrality of native wages to immigration is primarily due to three reasons. First, migrants and native workers are imperfect substitutes, so in most cases they do not compete for the same jobs (Manacorda et al., 2012). Second, the stories that low-skilled native workers choose to ignore are about the general equilibrium effects on their own income. Most of the spending of migrants remains in the local economy, thereby raising the demand for low-skilled services. Third, immigrants are not always employees; many start new firms and recent evidence suggests that those firms are, on average, more productive than local firms (Brown et al., 2019). However, overall, the low-skilled native worker does not feel economic benefits from migration, even though they do exist on an aggregate level. At the same time, there is a non-economic reason they vote for extreme parties: the identity costs imposed on them outweigh the economic benefits of immigration. Thus, the distinction of the rationale behind the extreme vote among the high-skilled and low-skilled fits within the treatments of populism as a tool to construct conflicting identities (Laclau, 2005).

In sum, high-skilled and low-skilled native workers can be exposed to migration in similar ways. The identity costs immigration imposes on them can be similar. However, it is the difference in the way the two groups experience the economic benefits from immigration that drives the difference in their political preferences to migrant inflows. This tilts low-skilled workers to the extreme, with some political economy models predicting greater support for far-right parties favoring more immigration controls (Llavador and Solano-García, 2011), and greater support for far-left redistribution policies (Ortega, 2010).

Are there immigration policy choices to address identity concerns? Recent literature has addressed the existence of optimal immigration policies in the presence of redistribution and social welfare benefits favoring native workers. Using a general equilibrium model of an economy with migrants of varying skill levels, Guerreiro et al. (2019) show the existence of *two optimal immigration policies*. Those optima depend on the local institutional environment with respect to the design of the social welfare system. The social welfare system may be designed so that immigrants benefit from it exactly as natives. Alternatively, immigrants may be denied access to the system. (Guerreiro et al. (2019) demonstrate that if immigrants have no access to the welfare system, then free immigration is optimal. However, when the local social welfare system does not discriminate between immigrants and natives, it is optimal to ban low-skilled immigration and open free immigration for high-skilled workers (p. 31) only. The recent policy proposals for a points-based system in the UK *à la* Canada and Australia reflect the fact that perhaps developed countries are indeed moving towards one of those two optima.

To our analysis, this result implies that antagonistic political agendas may flourish by creating a more robust feeling of identity among the members of a certain nation – a premise which necessarily requires an embodiment of otherness. The easiest to sell politically is, naturally, the group of immigrants, irrespective of how diverse this group is. This is why the *us-against-them* rhetoric works so well, particularly for voters who feel threatened by immigrants. This argument can be very smoothly pushed to the far-right: the very survival of a certain society depends on drawing a red line between *us* – the pure people – and *them*, who necessarily threaten our identity.

The threat from immigration in an already consolidated European democracy creates a different type of political preference than in Latin America because of identity differences between migrants and natives. Mukand and Rodrik (2015) use the differences in Latin American and European populism to build a political economy model along identity politics. The model illustrates how those two brands of populism – the far-left in Latin America and the far-right in Europe – could emerge within a liberal democracy. This goes beyond the limits of political science (Abromeit, 2017, p. 182), in which more recent contributions shed light on the ways some parties adopt extreme platforms to gain future votes (Eguia and Giovannoni, 2019).

The recent political economy literature offers additional approaches to explaining supply-side populism arising from identity concerns. For example, Voss (2018) uses labor market dualization – the fact that policies and reforms are designed to benefit insiders at the expense of outsider groups in the labor market – to explain why a similar labor market reform enacted in Germany and Spain has led to the emergence of right-wing populism in the former and of left-wing populism in the latter. His intuition is that traditional social democratic parties no longer represent a homogeneous class of voters. In turn, this leads to policy choices that disregard relevant segments of the traditional social democratic constituencies.

The ignorance of the traditional electorate, and a concurrent shift to an extreme platform, may be thought of as an investment in future votes at the expense of electoral losses in the immediate election cycle, a phenomenon described as *tactical extremism* (Eguia and Giovannoni, 2019). If the more extreme platform argues that certain shocks will materialize, and indeed they do, then the party will profit from the shift to the extreme. The model by Eguia and Giovannoni (2019) is potent in explaining the return of the Labour Party in the UK to a more extreme left rhetoric, and the refocusing of the Conservative party on a hard Brexit. It also provides insights into similar patterns in the USA and elsewhere (Wood et al., 2018), driven by both identity and socio-economic shocks. The next section reviews the recent literature on how the state of the economy affects populist votes, and how it amplifies the impact of identity shocks.

2.3 Economy

Apart from identity shocks, the state of the economy plays a pivotal role in populist votes. Guiso et al. (2017) discuss the broad implications of economic conditions for voter turnout and for the observed allocation of votes at the political fringes. Overall, economic insecurity directly affects turnout incentives and then pushes voters to the extremes. At the same time, there are indirect effects of economic insecurity to take into account, which run through voter trust in the economic system and mistrust of immigrants.

Overall, economic insecurity, however, is not sufficiently specific. We can group politically relevant economic shocks into two broad classes: globalization shocks and locally generated shocks. Globalization shocks are related to the distributive effects of trade, financial, and labor market openness. Locally generated shocks come not only from recessions, but also from the way governments respond to the need to provide social safety nets for the losers of recessions and globalization, e.g. fiscal expansion, or austerity.

Rodrik (2018) relates the emergence of various types of populism to economic policy reforms and business cycle shocks, particularly those related to globalization, which typically originate in large developed economies (Monnet and Puy, 2019). Once the shocks are transmitted elsewhere, they become politically relevant at the local level. For example, left-wing populism has emerged in Latin America due to recurrent cycles of trade and financial liberalization which increase the likelihood of financial crises (Mendoza and Quadrini, 2010) and prompt deep recessions in environments with traditionally toxic levels of income inequality. In turn, this creates masses of losers of globalization who demand large-scale redistribution platforms (Sachs, 1989). In contrast, right-wing populism has emerged in Western Europe and the USA because, there, globalization is manifested differently than in Latin America for three reasons: import competition (Autor, Dorn, and Hanson, 2016; Che et al., 2016), rising income inequality (Pastor and Veronesi, 2018), and immigration (Fetzer, 2012; Lazaridis and Wadia, 2015).

There is now an abundant literature on how economic crises affect extreme votes, especially since the Great Recession. In a review article which plays down the role of identity and other cultural factors, Guriev (2018) reviews the role of economic shocks. Based on earlier work by Algan et al. (2017), Guriev (2018) argues that rising unemployment caused an increase in populist votes after the Great Recession. Varaine (2018) expands the time span of the above works and focuses on longer-term patterns of radical votes in France, while Ferkiss (1962) discusses the trends in American extreme political preferences before the 1960s, and their shift from the far-left to the far-right. Glaeser (2005) provides further evidence of longer-term voter radicalization, and Varaine (2018) concludes that recessions and income inequality can play a decisive role in triggering and driving the dynamics of long-term extreme political preferences.

Further large-scale evidence demonstrates that recessions are among the most salient issues in affecting populist preferences. In an empirical work covering 90 elections across 16 European countries from 1990 to 2016, Rao et al. (2018) point to a large direct effect of recessions on voter polarization. Their results echo earlier studies on the period around the Great Depression, which have shown that economic slowdowns before elections are significantly correlated with extreme votes (de Bromhead et al., 2013).

Empirical work on crises and populist votes has also been done at the regional level within a country. The advantage of a within-country study is that it can isolate the impact of relevant economic shocks from the regional effects. This can be done because the distributions of identities within regions of the same country are often more or less identical, especially in a relatively homogenous society. This is what Bó et al. (2018) do for Sweden. They find that politicians in extreme parties are more likely to come from regions that have been hit harder by recessions (a supply-side effect on political platforms), and that the share of votes for extreme parties in those regions are also higher (a demand-side effect).

Economic shocks matter because they have differing distributional consequences across societal groups. Therefore, economic shocks impose changes to the identity rents of various groups within a society. For example, objective income inequality dynamics are a function of the state of the economy, and at the same time affect how the poor, the middle class, and the rich perceive themselves as opposed to the others. This can create antagonistic narratives between groups (Redbird and Grusky, 2016). This is because a recession typically hits low-skilled workers harder than the high-skilled (Matsaganis and Leventi, 2014). Low-skilled workers then experience a deeper relative deprivation. Consequently, the low-skilled will increasingly mobilize for parties representing their group interests, which may be far-left where economic shocks dominate, and far-right where the dominant shocks are on their identity. Thus, economic shocks become more politically relevant for groups that have been hit harder. As those groups become more sensitive to out-group threats in times of adverse economic shocks (Meuleman et al., 2019; Schlueter et al., 2013), a recession is expected to amplify the effects on extreme votes we observe from migration and inequality. Therefore, even if recessions may exert a weak direct effect on extreme votes (Stankov, 2018), evidence from a number of developed democracies suggests that they may indeed affect identity-based votes by influencing *perceptions* of societal decline (Davis et al., 2019).

Further, Guriev (2018) contends that the skill composition of trade matters to political approval for incumbent governments. Skilled workers approve incumbent governments more when the country exports more goods with skilled input. They disapprove more when the country imports more goods with skilled inputs – a conclusion based on an earlier work by Aksoy et al. (2018). The intuition for the above result is simple: more exports of skilled output means higher income for the skilled workers. Because the skilled input is provided by skilled workers, the skilled workers approve of globalization and, for example, EU integration. At the same time, because the unskilled workers are on the losing end of the distribution of the gains, they prefer more social protections (Lü et al., 2012), and cast more votes for Eurosceptic and anti-globalization political platforms.

Thus, the state of the economy creates and nurtures identity conflicts, which in turn play a key role in determining preferences for economic policies. Two recent papers (Grossman and Helpman, 2018; Shayo, 2020) formalize the intuition behind the impact. To illustrate the interplay between identity and the state of the economy on political preferences for trade policies, Grossman and Helpman (2018) develop a model in which voters care about their material satisfaction from consumption, but also about their identity rents: the benefits they derive from the fact that the groups they identify with are doing well, versus the "dissonance costs" of belonging to a group whose behavioral norms vary from their own. Thus, a society's welfare is defined not only by the sum of its individual members' material well-being, but also by their identity rents.

Echoing a classic argument from international trade economics, the optimal policy in the absence of identity rents is a zero tariff policy (free trade). However, the existence of identity rents changes the optimal trade policies. This happens because of the differing effects of trade liberalization on income across the skill distribution. As a result, the working class may cease to identify with the nation as a whole entity which also includes the rich elite, and begin to identify itself with the group of workers alone. Workers may experience this identification regime change for several reasons: a growing dissonance cost of being associated with those in a different income class; skill-biased technological progress which increases the wage gap between the rich and the poor; and improvements in terms-of-trade which result in a similar wage disparity (Grossman and Helpman, 2018, p. 17).

In other words, the skill gap drives an economic wedge between the rich and the poor, which can alter the identity costs of the working class sufficiently to cause them to undergo an identification regime change: a rejection of the legitimacy of the elites, and a dissociation from a broad version of the national identity, which they now limit to their fellow members of the working class (Grossman and Helpman, 2018, p. 17). Once the identification regime change is underway, policies that are optimal for a united nation with a common identity are no longer optimal. There exists a strictly non-zero tariff rate which improves the welfare of the poor. As in other works reviewed here, it is optimal for the poor working class to demand less globalization and higher tariffs.

Trade-induced shifts in voter preferences have been a topic of extensive empirical work. Just as theory predicts, trade shocks affect demand for trade protection. Autor, Dorn, Hanson, and Majlesi (2016) and Che et al. (2016) review the evidence for the USA. They find a robust effect of import competition on voter polarization and on demand for trade policy restrictions and economic assistance programs. These effects are in line with findings from the early literature of the political economy of reforms (Greskovits, 1993), as well as with evidence that voter support for free trade is a function of expected adjustment assistance (Lake and Millimet, 2016). Similarly to the conclusions for the USA, Dippel et al. (2015) find sufficient causal evidence of trade-induced shifts in voter preferences for the far-right parties in Germany, and Caselli et al. (2019) conduct a similar exercise for Italy. Recent evidence from 15 Western European nations confirms these preference shifts on a larger scale (Colantone and Stanig, 2018). It should be noted, however, that demands for trade protection are not always conditioned on disparities in skills or education. Di Tella and Rodrik (2019) conduct an online experiment in which trade shocks result in more protectionism among both low- and high-skilled workers.

The reasons for protectionist shifts in policy preferences can be traced back to labor market adjustments triggered by rising import competition. Those adjustments are dubbed *the China syndrome*: "Rising imports cause higher unemployment, lower labor force participation, and reduced wages in local labor markets that house import-competing manufacturing industries. In our main specification, import competition explains one-quarter of the contemporaneous aggregate decline in US manufacturing employment" (Autor et al., 2013, p. 2121). The import-competition shock is not only large but also long-lasting: wages and labor-force participation rates remain depressed and unemployment rates remain elevated for at least a full decade after the trade shock (Autor, Dorn, and Hanson, 2016, p. 205).

In sum, adverse economic shocks caused by policy liberalization trigger distributional changes in welfare which affect identity rents. In this section, we have considered how the interplay between identity rents and economic shocks deliver a politically relevant shift in voter preferences to the extreme. However, we have not yet considered the impacts of inequality of opportunity, income, and wealth on the formation of those rents. Section 2.4 discusses these.

2.4 Fairness

If identity becomes a more salient feature of voter preferences in times of economic distress, what affects identity? The issue has been raised by Kevane (1997), who argues that, while some identity traits are constant (e.g. skin color), others are subject to personal choice and by implication, subject to change. As the choice of identity is politically relevant, it is useful to explore what can change it. Our understanding of identity transformations, or the *dynamics of endogenous identity*, is still in the nascent stages (Besley and Persson, 2019; Collier, 2019a), but is a promising avenue for work due to its potential to explain the formation of political preferences.

In an exciting recent work, Bosworth and Snower (2019) explain individual identity formation as a function of one's abilities. They assume the existence of three types of identities: individualistic, communitarian, and multi-affiliated. People with an individualistic identity pursue egocentric values (e.g. consumption, status) and care less about their attachment to most groups. People with communitarian identities derive more utility from participating in groups than from their individual consumption or status rank. Multi-identity people pursue both individualistic and altruistic values, and their identity can morph into an individualistic or a communitarian identity.

A key assumption in the above work is that identity is fluid, and people choose their identity (and change it) based on which type gives them higher overall satisfaction in life. At the same time, one's abilities underlie the relative value of each type of identity for individual utility. Then, Bosworth and Snower (2019) explain, abilities determine the choice of identity: high-ability people care more about individual consumption and ultimately end up adopting individualistic identities, while low-ability people care more about group attachment, and adopt communitarian identities. Having adopted group-specific behavioral prescriptions, however, people find switching between identities very costly (Kevane, 1997, p. 2), in line with the social norms literature (Shayo, 2020; Williamson, 2000).

How is this relevant to the relationship between fairness and populism? Ability levels not only determine a person's identity but also their social status and position on the income ladder. Thus, an identity conflict between the elite and the poor will be more pronounced in a more unequal society: "the elite's rising preoccupation with individualistic material goals is matched by a rising preoccupation of the underprivileged with communitarian goals" (Bosworth and Snower, 2019, p. 20). So, abilities determine both income and the value divergence. Widening divergence in income and value then thins the identity center, and cements the differences between the two fragmented identity types: the elite, and the people.

Consequently, income differences become an important factor for identity formation. In a recent work, Collier (2019a) outlines the underlining mechanism. His starting position is that both the elite and the people care about two salient characteristics of identity: their nation, and their occupation. Once the elite start to become richer, they rationally reject some salient features they used to care about – e.g. their shared national identity with low-wage workers –and become more interested in the characteristics of their own jobs. As a result, they reduce their political support for redistribution favoring below-median earners, while at the same time low-wage workers increase their demands for it. Thus, similarly to Besley and Persson (2019), the model delivers a class cleavage along inequality-driven differences in identity, in contrast with other recent work that derives those cleavages from constant identity traits (Chua, 2018).

Even in the absence of identity issues, class fragmentation along the lines of substantive and procedural fairness can directly affect subsequent economic policies. This is because higher inequality increases demand for both anti-globalization and redistribution policies. Pastor and Veronesi (2018) illustrate the mechanism using voters who care not only about their level of consumption, but also about the level of inequality. In their model, a populist delivers lower consumption, but also lower inequality. Notice, however, that richer countries also consume more, which means they can afford to sacrifice some part of their consumption for more equality. As the marginal utility of consumption at high levels of consumption is low, voters in richer countries are more willing to make this sacrifice. In a constantly growing economy which continually increases income inequality, a populist offering a backlash against globalization and a redistribution policy to lower inequality eventually gets elected, with the richer countries becoming more vulnerable to this type of selection. This is what Pastor and Veronesi (2018) also observe in the data: extreme parties and platforms have recently gained most traction in developed countries.

In response to the potential threat of a backlash, an incumbent government has two choices: redistribution or neo-liberalism (Leon, 2014). On the one hand, it can offer a direct redistribution of consumption from the elites to the people through taxation and transfers. As transferring welfare to the bottom layers of the income distribution is able to disproportionately help them escape poverty and restore the feeling of fairness (Nolan and Thewisseng, 2019), this seems like a viable political strategy in theory.

In practice, however, the redistribution strategy is limited for three reasons. First, not everyone with a low-wage job will readily accept social transfers, especially in an environment of declining unionization (Jacobs and Myers, 2014; Macdonald, 2019). Labor unions are often able to influence the political preferences of their members (Kim and Margalit, 2017), but a general decline in union membership means that their influence is less relevant today than it has ever been in the post-World War II period. As a result, transfers may not generate an elastic voter response. Second, income transfers from the rich to the poor may deliver political self-harm, particularly for conservative governments, as they must reduce the consumption of their own base voters to accomplish it. Third, the government can also be accused of engaging in the type of macroeconomic populism that has consistently failed in Latin America (Dornbusch and Edwards, 1991; Sachs, 1989).

In contrast, if redistribution policies are hard to sell, the government can formulate a neo-liberal trickle-down policy – lower taxation for corporations and rich individuals in the hope that the additional welfare gains for the rich will find their way to low-paid workers. This is desirable for the rich, but is problematic for the poor. The difficulty with a trickle-down policy gaining widespread voter support in the post-GFC world is that trickle-down economics no longer works. Indeed, Reaganomics and Thatcherism drew their policies from a right-wing ideology, later mimicked elsewhere through global economic policy convergence (Stankov, 2017b). Those policies initially delivered for the poor as well as for the rich (Matthews and Minford, 1987; Samuelson, 1984), albeit with an emphasis placed squarely on the rich (Buchele, 1984; Jacobs and Myers, 2014). Today, however, trickle-down policies have effectively morphed into *trickle-back* policies, in which the additional welfare for the rich is fed back to the rich themselves, rather than being shared with low-skilled, low-paid workers. Why?

The reason is three-fold: tax loopholes, share buybacks, and real estate. First, local tax laws create loopholes which only rich individuals and firms can reasonably exploit to minimize their tax outlays. Second, tax breaks for corporations increase the demand for buybacks of their own stocks. This creates additional welfare only for those who have equity in the corporations in the first place (Lazonick, 2016; Ryoo, 2016). As the large majority of workers do not hold stocks, they are disenfranchised. Finally, if given a tax incentive, wealthy individuals and corporations do not spend much more on consumption goods. Rather, they invest the additional income in real estate, stocks, and bonds. However, who owns real estate, stocks, and bonds? It is the same class of people: *the elite*. Therefore, it can be argued that a trickle-down policy is designed by the elite for the elite, and therefore feeds voter polarization.

Real estate is a politically sensitive factor for voters for another reason: rental expenditures generally constitute a significant share of total household expenditures, especially for households at the bottom end of the income distribution (Dustmann et al., 2018). As home prices and rental rates are positively correlated, an increase in home prices drags rental rates upwards with them, and sways new cohorts of voters away from home ownership into renting (Joyce et al., 2017). Thus, a government policy that helps the rich spend more, including more on real estate, directly affects disposable worker income after rental payments. Low-skilled workers need to work ever harder to catch up with their previous level of consumption, which is unattainable, or move to lower quality accommodation. Even when low-skilled workers respond by supplying more hours of work, those will still be at the same low-paying jobs. As a result, "the income share of housing expenditures rises disproportionately for the bottom income quintile and falls for the top quintile" (Dustmann et al., 2018, p. 1), consistent with evidence from the beginning of the 20th century (Davis and Ortalo-Magné, 2011, p. 258). As the income share of rentals declines with income, the class fragmentation along income inequality becomes cemented. Thus, both procedural (policies) and substantive (resulting income) unfairness bolsters class divisions, which nourishes political fragmentation and voter polarization.

Empirical studies have broadly confirmed that fairness concerns of voters are politically consequential. Gidron and Hall (2020) find that social marginalization of voters is associated with a rise in extreme votes for both far-left and far-right parties, and with a decline in support for traditional mainstream parties, a conclusion which is re-examined in Chapter 3. As expected, the voters who are more vulnerable to social marginalization are those with lower incomes and education levels, who were quietly mobilizing in the US until the GFC made the election of Donald Trump possible (Komlos, 2018). Yet, as predicted by the Besley and Persson (2019) framework, fairness concerns are not a sufficient condition for voter polarization. Even in relatively equitable Switzerland, which is among the richest countries in Europe, voter polarization is high, not necessarily because of social or economic concerns, but because of identity issues, as outlined in a comparative study of voter polarization in Western democracies by Gidron, Adams, and Horne (2019) and by Norris and Inglehart (2019).

Ultimately, it is difficult to refute the joint significance of inequality and identity, especially with their varying significance along the stages of the business cycle. Similar to the analysis in Chapter 3, some empirical studies approach the correlation between extreme votes and inequality in a panel framework. For example, Han (2016) finds that income inequality has an explicit impact on far-right votes. This effect is also different across groups with different skills, conforming to the theoretical arguments above.

In addition to the skill levels of voters, their age also matters in how they respond to inequality when casting a ballot. Using data from European regions, (Winkler, 2019, p. 137) finds that rising inequality delivers more of both far-left and far-right votes, but the effect on far-right votes is significant for older individuals and difficult to disentangle from the effect of salient anti-immigrant sentiments among older voters. Huber and Oberdabernig (2016) also conclude that pro-immigration attitudes weaken as the age of the native voters becomes higher.

The body of theoretical and empirical literature reviewed above point to joint salience of inequality and identity in voter polarization, especially in times of economic distress. Chapter 3 reduces those theories to testable hypotheses and finds evidence in their favor. It also produces some novel results which have not been explored in the literature to date.

Bibliography

Abromeit, J. (2017). A critical review of recent literature on populism. *Politics and Governance*, 5(4), 177–186.

Acemoglu, D., & Robinson, J. A. (2001). A theory of political transitions. *American Economic Review, 91*(4), 938–963.

Akerlof, G. A., & Kranton, R. E. (2000). Economics and identity. *The Quarterly Journal of Economics, 115*(3), 715–753.

Aksoy, C. G., Guriev, S., & Treisman, D. S. (2018). Globalization, government popularity, and the great skill divide. Working Paper 25062, National Bureau of Economic Research.

Alabrese, E., Becker, S. O., Fetzer, T., & Novy, D. (2019). Who voted for Brexit? Individual and regional data combined. *European Journal of Political Economy, 56*, 132–150.

Algan, Y., Guriev, S., Papaioannou, E., & Passari, E. (2017). The European trust crisis and the rise of populism. *Brookings Papers on Economic Activity*, 309–382.

Autor, D., Dorn, D., Hanson, G., and Majlesi, K. (2016). Importing political polarization? The electoral consequences of rising trade exposure. Working Paper 22637, National Bureau of Economic Research.

Autor, D. H., Dorn, D., & Hanson, G. H. (2013). The China syndrome: Local labor market effects of import competition in the United States. *American Economic Review, 103*(6), 2121–2168.

Autor, D. H., Dorn, D., & Hanson, G. H. (2016). The China shock: Learning from labor-market adjustment to large changes in trade. *Annual Review of Economics, 8*(1), 205–240.

Becker, S. O., Fetzer, T., & Novy, D. (2017). Who voted for Brexit? A comprehensive district-level analysis. *Economic Policy, 32*(92), 601–650.

Bernstein, M. (2005). Identity politics. *Annual Review of Sociology, 31*(1), 47–74.

Bértoa, F. C., & Weber, T. (2019). Restrained change: Party systems in times of economic crisis. *The Journal of Politics, 81*(1), 233–245.

Besley, T., & Persson, T. (2019). The rise of identity politics. Working Paper, London School of Economics.

Betz, H.-G. (1993). The two faces of radical right-wing populism in Western Europe. *The Review of Politics, 55*(4), 663–685.

Blanchard, E., & Willmann, G. (2011). Escaping a protectionist rut: Policy mechanisms for trade reform in a democracy. *Journal of International Economics, 85*(1), 72–85.

Bó, E. D., Finan, F., Folke, O., Persson, T., & Rickne, J. (2018). Economic losers and political winners: Sweden's radical right. Working Paper, Association of Swedish Development Economists. Mimeo.

Bosworth, S. J., & Snower, D. J. (2019). The interplay of economic, social and political fragmentation. Working Paper SM-WP-2019-011, Blavatnik School of Government, University of Oxford.

Boucekkine, R., Prieur, F., & Puzon, K. (2016). On the timing of political regime changes in resource-dependent economies. *European Economic Review, 85*, 188–207.

Brennan, G., & Buchanan, J. (1984). Voter choice: Evaluating political alternatives. *American Behavioral Scientist, 28*(2), 185–201.

Brown, J. D., Earle, J. S., Kim, M. J., & Lee, K. M. (2019). Immigrant entrepreneurs and innovation in the U.S. high-tech sector. Working Paper 25565, National Bureau of Economic Research.

Buchele, R. (1984). Reaganomics and the fairness issue. *Challenge, 27*(4), 25–31.

Caselli, M., Fracasso, A., & Traverso, S. (2020). Globalization and electoral outcomes: Evidence from Italy. *Economics and Politics, 32*(1), 68–103. Published online on 2 October 2019.

Center for Systemic Peace. (2019). Polity IV project, political regime characteristics and transitions, 1800–2018. Retrieved October 15, 2019 from http://www.systemicpeace.org

Che, Y., Lu, Y., Pierce, J. R., Schott, P. K., & Tao, Z. (2016). Does trade liberalization with China influence U.S. elections? Working Paper 22178, National Bureau of Economic Research.

Chua, A. (2018). *Political tribes: Group instinct and the fate of nations.* Bloomsbury Publishing.

Colantone, I., & Stanig, P. (2018). The trade origins of economic nationalism: Import competition and voting behavior in Western Europe. *American Journal of Political Science, 62*(4), 936–953.

Collier, P. (2019a). Diverging identities: A model of class formation. Working Paper SM-WP-2019–01, Blavatnik School of Government, University of Oxford.

Collier, P. (2019b). Rational social man and the compliance problem: An application of identity economics. Working Paper SM-WP-2019-03, Blavatnik School of Government, University of Oxford.

Dalio, R., Kryger, S., Rogers, J., & Davis, G. (2017). Populism: The phenomenon. Technical Report 3/22/2017, Bridgewater Associates, LP.

Davis, M. A., & Ortalo-Magné, F. (2011). Household expenditures, wages, rents. *Review of Economic Dynamics, 14*(2), 248–261.

Davis, N., Goidel, K., Lipsmeyer, C., Whitten, G., & Young, C. (2019). Economic vulnerability, cultural decline, and nativism: Contingent and indirect effects. *Social Science Quarterly, 100*(2), 430–446.

de Bromhead, A., Eichengreen, B., & O'Rourke, K. H. (2013). Political extremism in the 1920s and 1930s: Do German lessons generalize? *The Journal of Economic History, 73*(2), 371–406.

Di Tella, R., & Rodrik, D. (2019). Labor market shocks and the demand for trade protection: Evidence from online surveys. Working Paper 25705, National Bureau of Economic Research.

Dippel, C., Gold, R., & Heblich, S. (2015). Globalization and its (dis-)content: Trade shocks and voting behavior. Working Paper 21812, National Bureau of Economic Research.

Dornbusch, R., & Edwards, S. (1990). Macroeconomic populism. *Journal of Development Economics, 32*(2), 247–277.

Dornbusch, R., & Edwards, S. (1991). *The macroeconomics of populism in Latin America.* University of Chicago Press.

Downs, A. (1957). An economic theory of political action in a democracy. *Journal of Political Economy, 65*(2), 135–150.

Dustmann, C., Fitzenberger, B., & Zimmermann, M. (2018). Housing expenditures and income inequality. IZA Discussion Papers 11953, Institute of Labor Economics (IZA).

Dustmann, C., & Frattini, T. (2014). The fiscal effects of immigration to the UK. *The Economic Journal, 124*(580), F593–F643.

Edo, A., Giesing, Y., Öztunc, J., & Poutvaara, P. (2019). Immigration and electoral support for the far-left and the far-right. *European Economic Review, 115,* 99–143.

Edwards, S. (2019). On Latin American populism, and its echoes around the world. *Journal of Economic Perspectives, 33*(4), 76–99.

Eguia, J. X., & Giovannoni, F. (2019). Tactical extremism. *American Political Science Review, 113*(1), 282–286.

Facchini, G., & Steinhardt, M. F. (2011). What drives U.S. immigration policy? Evidence from congressional roll call votes. *Journal of Public Economics, 95*(7), 734–743.

Ferkiss, V. C. (1962). Political and intellectual origins of American radicalism, right and left. *The Annals of the American Academy of Political and Social Science, 344*(1), 1–12.

Fetzer, J. S. (2012). Public opinion and populism. In M. R. Rosenblum & D. J. Tichenor (Eds.), *Oxford handbook of the politics of international migration.* Oxford University Press. DOI: 10.1093/oxfordhb/9780195337228.013.0013

Friedberg, R. M., & Hunt, J. (1995). The impact of immigrants on host country wages, employment and growth. *Journal of Economic Perspectives, 9*(2), 23–44.

Galiani, S., & Torrens, G. (2014). Autocracy, democracy and trade policy. *Journal of International Economics, 93*(1), 173–193.

Gaston, N., & Rajaguru, G. (2013). International migration and the welfare state revisited. *European Journal of Political Economy, 29,* 90–101.

Geddes, B. (1999). What do we know about democratization after twenty years? *Annual Review of Political Science, 2*(1), 115–144.

Gidron, N., & Bonikowski, B. (2013). Varieties of populism: Literature review and research agenda. Technical Report 13-0004, Weatherhead Center.

Gidron, N., & Hall, P. A. (2020). Populism as a problem of social integration. *Comparative Political Studies, 53*(7), 1027–1059.

Gidron, N., Adams, J., & Horne, W. (2019). Toward a comparative research agenda on affective polarization in mass publics. *APSA Comparative Politics Newsletter, 29,* 30–36.

Giordani, P. E., & Mariani, F. (2019). Unintended consequences: Can the rise of the educated class explain the revival of protectionism? Technical Report, LUISS University of Rome; Catholic University of Louvain. Mimeo.

Glaeser, E. L. (2005). The political economy of hatred. *The Quarterly Journal of Economics, 120*(1), 45–86.

Greskovits, B. (1993). The use of compensation in economic adjustment programmes. *Acta Oeconomica, 45*(1/2), 43–68.

Gros, C. (2017). Entrenched time delays versus accelerating opinion dynamics: Are advanced democracies inherently unstable? *The European Physical Journal. Part B, 90*(11), 223.

Grossman, G. M., & Helpman, E. (2018). Identity politics and trade policy. Working Paper 25348, National Bureau of Economic Research.

Guerreiro, J., Rebelo, S., & Teles, P. (2019). What is the optimal immigration policy? Migration, jobs and welfare. Working Paper 26154, National Bureau of Economic Research.

Guiso, L., Herrera, H., Morelli, M., & Sonno, T. (2017). Populism: Demand and supply. Discussion Papers Series 11871, Centre for Economic Policy Research.

Guriev, S. (2018). Economic drivers of populism. *AEA Papers and Proceedings, 108*, 200–203.

Hainmueller, J., & Hopkins, D. J. (2014). Public attitudes toward immigration. *Annual Review of Political Science, 17*(1), 225–249.

Hainmueller, J., Hiscox, M. J., & Margalit, Y. (2015). Do concerns about labor market competition shape attitudes toward immigration? New evidence. *Journal of International Economics, 97*(1), 193–207.

Halla, M., Wagner, A. F., & Zweimüller, J. (2017). Immigration and voting for the far right. *Journal of the European Economic Association, 15*(6), 1341–1385.

Han, K. J. (2016). Income inequality and voting for radical right-wing parties. *Electoral Studies, 42*, 54–64.

Huber, P., & Oberdabernig, D. A. (2016). The impact of welfare benefits on natives' and immigrants' attitudes toward immigration. *European Journal of Political Economy, 44*, 53–78.

Iturbe-Ormaetxe, I., & Romero, J. G. (2016). Financing public goods and attitudes toward immigration. *European Journal of Political Economy, 44*, 159–178.

Jacobs, D., & Myers, L. (2014). Union strength, neoliberalism, and inequality: Contingent political analyses of U.S. income differences since 1950. *American Sociological Review, 79*(4), 752–774.

Jolly, S. K., & DiGiusto, G. M. (2014). Xenophobia and immigrant contact: French public attitudes toward immigration. *The Social Science Journal, 51*(3), 464–473.

Joyce, R., Mitchell, M., & Keiller, A. N. (2017). The cost of housing for low-income renters. Report 132, Institute for Fiscal Studies.

Karakas, L. D., & Mitra, P. D. D. (2019). Immigration policy in the presence of identity politics. Technical Report, Syracuse University.

Karapin, R. (1998). Explaining far-right electoral successes in Germany: The politicization of immigration-related issues. *German Politics and Society, 16*(3), 24–61.

Kendall-Taylor, A., Lindstaedt, N., & Frantz, E. (2019). *Democracies and authoritarian regimes.* Oxford University Press.

Kevane, M. (1997). Can there be an 'identity economics'? Working Paper, Santa Clara University.

Kim, S., & Margalit, Y. (2017). Informed preferences? The impact of unions on workers' policy views. *American Journal of Political Science, 61*(3), 728–743.

Komlos, J. (2018). The economic roots of the rise of Trumpism. CESifo Working Paper Series 6868, CESifo Group Munich.

Krastev, I. (2017). *After Europe*. University of Pennsylvania Press.

Krishnakumar, J., & Müller, T. (2012). The political economy of immigration in a direct democracy: The case of Switzerland. *European Economic Review*, *56*(2), 174–189.

Laclau, E. (2005). *On populist reason*. Phronesis Series. Verso.

Lake, J., & Millimet, D. L. (2016). An empirical analysis of trade-related redistribution and the political viability of free trade. *Journal of International Economics*, *99*, 156–178.

Lazaridis, G., & Wadia, K. (2015). *The securitisation of migration in the EU: Debates since 9/11*. The European Union in international affairs. Palgrave Macmillan UK.

Lazonick, W. (2016). How stock buybacks make Americans vulnerable to globalization. Working Paper, East-West Center.

Leon, G. (2014). Strategic redistribution: The political economy of populism in Latin America. *European Journal of Political Economy*, *34*, 39–51.

Llavador, H., & Solano-Garcia, A. (2011). Immigration policy with partisan parties. *Journal of Public Economics*, *95*(1), 134–142.

Lü, X., Scheve, K., & Slaughter, M. J. (2012). Inequity aversion and the international distribution of trade protection. *American Journal of Political Science*, *56*(3), 638–654.

Macdonald, D. (2019). Labor unions and support for redistribution in an era of inequality. *Social Science Quarterly*, *100*(4), 1197–1214.

Manacorda, M., Manning, A., & Wadsworth, J. (2012). The impact of immigration on the structure of wages: Theory and evidence from Britain. *Journal of the European Economic Association*, *10*(1), 120–151.

Matsaganis, M., & Leventi, C. (2014). The distributional impact of austerity and the recession in Southern Europe. *South European Society and Politics*, *19*(3), 393–412.

Matthews, K., & Minford, P. (1987). Mrs Thatcher's economic policies 1979–1987. *Economic Policy*, *2*(5), 57–101.

Mayda, A. M. (2006). Who is against immigration? A cross-country investigation of individual attitudes toward immigrants. *The Review of Economics and Statistics*, *88*(3), 510–530.

Mendoza, E. G., & Quadrini, V. (2010). Financial globalization, financial crises and contagion. *Journal of Monetary Economics*, *57*(1), 24–39. Carnegie-Rochester Conference Series on Public Policy: Credit Market Turmoil: Implications for Policy April 17–18, 2009.

Meuleman, B., Abts, K., Schmidt, P., Pettigrew, F., & Davidov, E. (2020). Economic conditions, group relative deprivation and ethnic threat perceptions: A cross-national perspective. *Journal of Ethnic and Migration Studies*, *46*(3), 593–611.

Monnet, E., & Puy, D. (2019). One ring to rule them all? New evidence on world cycles. Working Paper WP/19/202, International Monetary Fund.

Moriconi, S., Peri, G., & Turati, R. (2018). Skill of the immigrants and vote of the natives: Immigration and nationalism in European elections 2007–2016. Working Paper 25077, National Bureau of Economic Research.

Mudde, C., & Rovira Kaltwasser, C. (2011). Voices of the peoples: Populism in Europe and Latin America compared. Technical Report, Kellog Institute for International Studies.

Mudde, C., & Rovira Kaltwasser, C. (2017). *Populism: A very short introduction.* Oxford University Press.

Mukand, S., & Rodrik, D. (2015). The political economy of liberal democracy. Working Paper 21540, National Bureau of Economic Research.

Nolan, B., & Thewisseng, S. (2019). Inequality and real income growth for middle and low-income households across rich countries in recent decades. Working Paper SM-WP-2019-07, Blavatnik School of Government, University of Oxford.

Norris, P., & Inglehart, R. (2019). *Cultural backlash and the rise of populism: Trump, Brexit, and authoritarian populism.* Cambridge University Press.

Ocampo, E. (2015). Commodity price booms and populist cycles. an explanation of Argentina's decline in the 20th century. CEMA Working Papers: Serie Documentos de Trabajo. 562, Universidad del CEMA.

Ortega, F. (2010). Immigration, citizenship, and the size of government. *The B.E. Journal of Economic Analysis and Policy, 10*(1), published online.

Ortega, F., & Polavieja, J. G. (2012). Labor-market exposure as a determinant of attitudes toward immigration. *Labour Economics, 19*(3), 298–311.

Pastor, L., & Veronesi, P. (2018). Inequality aversion, populism, and the backlash against globalization. Working Paper 24900, National Bureau of Economic Research.

Poutvaara, P., & Steinhardt, M. F. (2018). Bitterness in life and attitudes towards immigration. *European Journal of Political Economy, 55*, 471–490.

Rao, M., Raschky, P. A., & Tombazos, C. G. (2018). Political extremism and economic activity. *Economics Letters, 170*, 59–62.

Redbird, B., & Grusky, D. B. (2016). Distributional effects of the Great Recession: Where has all the sociology gone? *Annual Review of Sociology, 42*(1), 185–215.

Riker, W. H., & Ordeshook, P. C. (1968). A theory of the calculus of voting. *The American Political Science Review, 62*(1), 25–42.

Rodrik, D. (2018). Populism and the economics of globalization. *Journal of International Business Policy, 1*(1), 12–33.

Romer, P. M. (1996). Preferences, promises, and the politics of entitlement. In V. R. Fuchs (Ed.), *Individual and social responsibility: Child care, education, medical care, and long-term care in America* (pp. 195–228). University of Chicago Press.

Ryoo, S. (2016). Inequality of income and wealth in the long run: A Kaldorian perspective. *Metroeconomica, 67*(2), 429–457.

Sachs, J. (1989). Social conflict and populist policies in Latin America. Working Paper 2897, National Bureau of Economic Research.

Samuelson, P. A. (1984). Evaluating Reaganomics. *Challenge, 27*(5), 4–11.

Scheve, K. F., & Slaughter, M. J. (2001). Labor market competition and individual preferences over immigration policy. *The Review of Economics and Statistics*, *83*(1), 133–145.

Schlueter, E., Meuleman, B., & Davidov, E. (2013). Immigrant integration policies and perceived group threat: A multilevel study of 27 Western and Eastern European countries. *Social Science Research*, *42*(3), 670–682.

Shayo, M. (2020). Social identity and economic policy. *Annual Review of Economics*, *12*. forthcoming.

Stankov, P. (2017a). Crises, welfare, and populism. In *Economic freedom and welfare before and after the crisis* (pp. 135–164). Cham: Springer International Publishing.

Stankov, P. (2017b). Policy convergence vs. welfare convergence. In *Economic freedom and welfare before and after the crisis* (pp. 69–97). Cham: Springer International Publishing.

Stankov, P. (2018). The political economy of populism: An empirical investigation. *Comparative Economic Studies*, *60*(2), 230–253.

Varaine, S. (2018). Bad times are not good times for revolutions: Collective deprivation and the mobilization level of French radical movements (1882–1980). *Journal of Community and Applied Social Psychology*, *28*(4), 258–271.

Voss, D. (2018). The political economy of European populism: Labour market dualisation and protest voting in Germany and Spain. Discussion Paper 132–2018, LEQS-LSE 'Europe in Question' Series, London School of Economics.

WID.World. (2019). The world inequality database. Retrieved October 5, 2019 from https://wid.world/

Williamson, O. E. (2000). The new institutional economics: Taking stock, looking ahead. *Journal of Economic Literature*, *38*(3), 595–613.

Winkler, H. (2019). The effect of income inequality on political polarization: Evidence from European regions, 2002–2014. *Economics and Politics*, *31*(2), 137–162.

Wood, D., Daley, J., & Chivers, C. (2018). Australia demonstrates the rise of populism is about more than economics. *Australian Economic Review*, *51*(3), 399–410.

3 Populist cycles
An illustrated history

The theory of populist cycles predicts that identity issues and socio-economic variables influence extreme voting patterns. As measures of identity considerations pose a methodological challenge, we leave the impact of those for future work. This chapter does address how inequality, immigration, and austerity leave a mark on extreme votes at both ends of the political spectrum. The chapter first presents graphical evidence illustrating the theories developed in Chapter 2. Then, more rigorous empirical tests are applied to examine what drives extreme voting cycles. Because votes in the extreme affect votes in the center, we simultaneously examine how macro-trends in inequality, immigration, and austerity correlate with centrist votes. Before analyzing the correlations, we need to further examine the data on political preferences.

3.1 The data on voting cycles and their correlates

The data on voting patterns in both Europe and Latin America has received well-deserved attention over the past few years. A few of the more comprehensive sources on developed countries are Döring and Manow (2019) and Heinö (2019). Data on Latin America has also been collected by Rode and Revuelta (2015), Stankov (2018), and Cachanosky and Padilla (2019), among others.

The most comprehensive dataset compiling electoral outcomes from the beginning of the 20th century has been produced by Döring and Manow (2019). It includes data on general elections for lower houses of national parliaments in all European Union (EU) and most OECD countries, as well as European Parliament elections after 1979. Coverage for democracies in Central and Eastern Europe begins around 1990, when the countries in the region abandoned their socialist experiments and initiated democratic elections. The coverage for the rest of the countries starts at the time of their democratic transition. The full country and time coverage of national and

Table 3.1 Country and Time Coverage in the *ParlGov* Data

Country	Time Coverage	Country	Time Coverage
Australia	1901–2016	Japan	1946–2017
Austria	1919–2019	Latvia	1990–2019
Belgium	1900–2019	Lithuania	1990–2019
Bulgaria	1991–2019	Luxembourg	1919–2019
Canada	1900–2015	Malta	1947–2019
Croatia	2000–2019	Netherlands	1918–2019
Cyprus	1976–2019	New Zealand	1902–2017
Czech Republic	1990–2019	Norway	1900–2017
Denmark	1901–2019	Poland	1989–2019
Estonia	1992–2019	Portugal	1975–2019
Finland	1917–2019	Romania	1990–2019
France	1902–2019	Slovakia	1990–2019
Germany	1919–2019	Slovenia	1990–2019
Greece	1974–2019	Spain	1977–2019
Hungary	1990–2019	Sweden	1911–2019
Iceland	1919–2017	Switzerland	1902–2015
Ireland	1922–2019	Turkey	1983–2018
Israel	1949–2019	United Kingdom	1918–2019
Italy	1946–2019		

Notes: The table lists the 37 countries in the *Elections* sheet of the Döring and Manow (2019) data, as well as its time coverage.

EU Parliament elections is given in Table 3.1. Due to its extensive coverage, the analysis below is based on the Döring and Manow (2019) data.

The *Elections* sheet in the Döring and Manow (2019) data records 8,478 individual vote shares for parties across the ideological spectrum. The ideology of each party is positioned on a Left–Right scale ranging from 0 to 10. The position is a simple average of the party positions in four studies of party positions and spaces: Castles and Mair (1984), Huber and Inglehart (1995), Benoit and Laver (2006), and Bakker et al. (2015). In essence, these studies survey local political system experts on the ideology of each electorally significant domestic party. Then, in line with Castles and Mair (1984, p. 87), the average of the expert scores for each party is mapped from the 0–10 Left–Right scale to five ideological domains as follows:

- 0–1.25: Far-Left;
- 1.26–3.75: Moderate Left (Center-Left);
- 3.76–6.25: Center;
- 6.26–8.75: Moderate Right (Center-Right);
- 8.76–10.00: Far-Right.

When each party has been assigned a score, we can add the vote shares within each ideological domain, and each electoral cycle in any country.

Thus, for any country and election cycle we can measure the electoral support for extreme, center-left, centrist, and center-right parties. In some countries, both parliamentary and EU elections are held within the same year. If we sum the votes cast in the national and EU parliamentary elections which were held in those years, vote shares for some ideological domains can reach higher than 100%. Therefore, for those years in which both national and supranational elections took place, we not only sum up the vote shares for each ideology, but also separate the electoral outcomes by election type. Next, we can drop the results for the EU elections to remain with the far-left and the far-right votes in each country cast in national elections.

Those observations are then matched with data on inequality and immigration patterns. The inequality data is taken from the *World Income Inequality Database* (*WIID*) *4.0* produced by UNU-WIDER (2018). The WIID provides extensive coverage of Gini coefficients, quantile and decile income ratios, and a novel measure of the income shares of the top and bottom 5% of the population. The inequality measures included in the analysis below are the Gini coefficient for each country-year, and the top-bottom 5% ratio, averaged across countries for each year, and then smoothed over 5-year periods to arrive at an overall trend in global income inequality. Other existing datasets cover similar periods and countries, e.g. Milanovic (2014) and WID.World (2019). We apply the WIID 4.0 data here due to its similarly extensive coverage and relative ease of use. However, we acknowledge that WID.World (2019) is superior in terms of coverage, as it features not only income, but also wealth inequality, and income ratios unavailable elsewhere.

Unlike the existence of multiple authoritative data sources on income inequality, the migration data is much scarcer, especially before the 1980s. Annual migration data exists only for OECD countries (OECD, 2019), and at 5-year intervals for the rest of the world (United Nations, 2019). As the data on electoral outcomes used here includes mostly OECD countries, using the OECD migration data seems reasonable. The most comprehensive source of long-term data on government expenditures for the same countries is the one by Jordà et al. (2017). This is used to capture patterns of austerity and fiscal expansions. Historical data on GDP per capita is produced by Bolt et al. (2018), which is used to gauge recessions in the sample used below.

The time-varying country-level electoral outcomes lend themselves to a panel study of extreme and centrist votes, which appears at the end of this chapter. The country-level election data allows for an aggregation within each year, so that we get a clearer notion of the overall voting cycles over time. Aggregation is done by averaging the results for each party ideology within each year across countries.

The overall trends in extreme voting (the total of far-left and far-right votes) are presented next, together with simultaneous trends in inequality and immigration. Then, a more detailed discussion of the far-left, far-right, and centrist vote patterns follows.

3.2 The long waves of extreme voting

Figure 3.1 presents a remarkable 120-year history of extreme voting. Three distinct periods – or long waves – are outlined in this history, each of which lasted approximately 35–40 years. The first period runs from the beginning of the 20th century until the depths of the Great Depression. In this period, populist, nationalist, and extreme votes in general rose sharply, particularly during World War I (WWI). The decade after WWI, a period known as the Roaring Twenties, placed a temporary brake on the rise of extremism, before the Depression re-fueled its momentum. The Great Depression brought about the highest rates of extremist voting in the modern democratic history of the world.

After the world had bottomed out from the Depression in the mid-1930s, an equally sharp demise of extreme voting took place until the end of the 1960s. The World War II (WWII) years and the first few post-war years were an exception from the trend, with a marked increase in extreme voting preferences. However, this break from the overall downward trend was short-lived, as Western Europe dealt with post-war devastation and embarked on its integration project in the late 1940s. The cycle of more centrist voting ended with the first wave of European Economic Community (EEC) enlargement when the UK, Ireland, and Denmark joined the EEC.

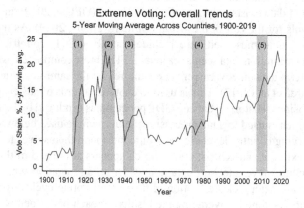

Figure 3.1 Extreme Voting: 1900–2019

The third long wave of extreme voting continues to date. Heinö (2019) documents a resurgence of total extreme votes from the beginning of the 1980s. However, the gradual resurgence of the extreme voting began a decade earlier. Interestingly, an increase in extreme voting can not only be observed around the first EEC enlargement; every enlargement since has spurred some extremist momentum, with notable hikes after 1981 when Greece joined, after 1986 when Spain and Portugal joined, and particularly after the most significant enlargement when 12 Central and Eastern European member states joined between 2004 and 2007. These observations are consistent with the hypothesis that European enlargement triggers nationalistic voter responses, manifested in a resurgence of the overall extreme vote.

The third wave of the extreme is more than just the longest one on record. The 2019 European Parliament elections also marked a high tide of extreme preferences not seen since the Great Depression. It is perhaps not a coincidence that the latest tide was preceded by the Global Financial Crisis (GFC) and the Eurozone crisis of 2009–2012.

Wars, economic crises, and waves of EU enlargement all prompt surges of extremism. However, they are insufficient to fully explain the cycles of populism pervading the last 120 years of Western democracy. In what follows, we focus on two factors which contribute to the story of populist cycles: income inequality and migration.

There are two measures of income inequality which both seem to correlate well with extreme votes, and lend themselves to measurement in a sufficient number of countries over time: the Gini coefficient, and a somewhat less often-used ratio of the top versus bottom 5% (TB-5). The Gini coefficient has an advantage in that it offers data on voting patterns covering nearly the entire 120-year period of electoral outcomes. Thus, we could correlate Gini with voting patterns for nearly the entire 120-year period, which is done in Figure 3.2.

Figure 3.2 is informative about the changeable dynamics between income inequality and extreme voting. Until the end of WWII, the correlation was mostly positive. As income inequality soared, extreme votes moved upward along with it. From the mid-1940s, however, the relationship changed, and the correlation became negative. In political science, this is explained by the changing "growth regimes" (Hopkin and Blyth, 2019). Hopkin and Blyth (2019, p. 194) argue that "the macroeconomic regime that governed the markets of the advanced capitalist democracies from the end of the Second World War until the mid-1970s produced a growth model that was particularly favorable to labor." This is because the mainstream parties of the post-WWII world competed for votes on the basis of public goods provision. However, the 1970s stagflation shifted the economic policy regime towards capital owners, which spurred inequalities, especially since the 1990s. Since

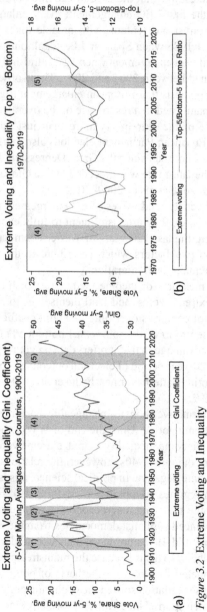

Figure 3.2 Extreme Voting and Inequality

the 1990s, the long-term trends in both income inequality and extreme voting have moved in tandem, as they did before WWII.

The positive association between the TB-5% income ratio and extreme voting is even stronger. After the mid-1970s stagflation – a period of high inflation accompanied by recessions – ended around 1980, the TB-5 ratio began moving in tandem with extreme voting. The correlation is particularly informative from the end of the 1980s. Periods of rapidly expanding income disparities were accompanied by boosts in extreme voting, and stagnating extreme voting – particularly between 1993 and 2006 – coexisted with a stagnating divergence of top-to-bottom income ratios. However, ever since the GFC spurred rapidly expanding income inequality across the developed world, extreme left and extreme right vote shares gradually doubled their total share.

The graphical evidence of the relationship between income inequality and extreme voting shows a positive association between the two. There is a similarly credible association between extreme voting and immigration.

The graphical association between extreme voting and immigration is presented in Figure 3.3. Four migration patterns are illustrated: foreign population inflow; net migration (inflow minus outflow); the number of foreign-born people already living in the country; and the number of asylum-seekers. The natural logarithm was taken of the absolute numbers to allow for more informative trend comparisons.

Figure 3.3(a) demonstrates that the inflow of migrants is a leading indicator of extreme votes. This is particularly visible in the mid-1980s, immediately before the GFC, and after the GFC. These were periods of large migrant inflows into old Western democracies, and are marked by robust increases in extreme voting. The relationship during the GFC seemingly breaks down: as the total of far-left and far-right voting crept up, migrant inflow stalled.

The co-movements of net migration and extreme voting are shown in Figure 3.3(b). The net inflow of migrants is the difference between the foreign inflow and the outflow of workers in a given economy. Whereas net migration was trending together with extreme votes in most of the two decades running up the GFC, it seems to have broken down in the few years prior to the GFC. However, net migration regained its concurrency with extreme voting immediately after the Euro crisis was resolved in 2012.

Similar correspondences can be drawn for the relationships between extreme voting and the other two foreign population measures in our data: the stock of foreign-born populations, and asylum-seekers. The two relationships are presented in Figure 3.3(c) and Figure 3.3(d), respectively. Neither changes the main message about migration: it is a powerful driver of extreme political preferences.

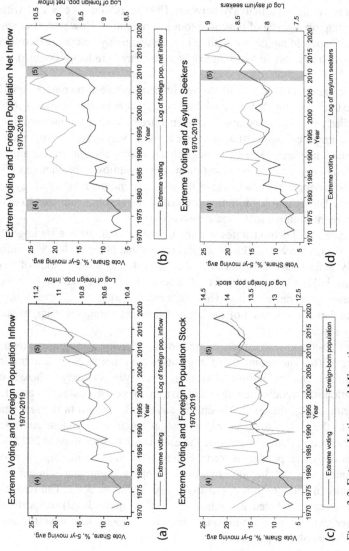

Figure 3.3 Extreme Voting and Migration

Although revealing *per se*, aggregated extreme preferences mask the underlying differences between the popularity of far-left and far-right political platforms. Those are presented in Section 3.3.

3.3 The far-left and the far-right: a closer look

A closer look at the far-left and the far-right suggests that the three long waves of extreme voting were driven mostly by the far-right vote. This is evident in Figure 3.4. Over the long run, the far-right vote experienced far larger swings than the far-left. Today, the far-left ideology is not significantly more popular than it was during the Great Depression, still commanding between 5–8% of the vote.

The similarity between far-left votes today and during the Great Depression does not mean that the far-left was immune to swings. The first significant jump in the popularity of the far-left came in the 1920s and ended with the Great Depression. Two factors may have contributed to this surge. First, the far-left communist ideology, which was being instated as official government policy in Russia, was making its way into the rest of Europe. Second, the generally strong economies of the late 1920s increased the bargaining power of labor, which the far-left tends to prioritize. The end of the Depression brought more centrist politicians into power, which curtailed the rise of the far-left.

The far-right suffered from the rise of the post-Depression centrist vote even more. Averaging about 15% during the Depression, the far-right contracted to a meagre 5% before WWII. However, just as WWI brought the far-right into mainstream politics, WWII marked an expansion of both extreme left and extreme right. After WWII, until around the beginning of

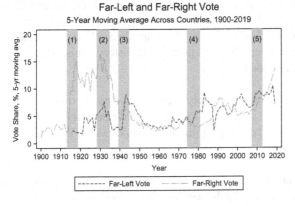

Figure 3.4 The Far-Left and the Far-Right: 1900–2019

the 1970s, extremist parties contracted to the political fringes. This was due to rapid post-war growth, declining income inequality, especially since the mid-1950s (see Figure 3.5), relatively closed labor markets, rising union power, and an overall expansion of the government's role in the economy, most visible in the establishment of many "cradle-to-grave" social welfare systems (Norris and Inglehart, 2019).

The rising unemployment and inflation of the late 1970s affected the poor most and brought labor discontent back to the fore. As a result, far-left parties gained electoral traction. As soon as stagflation ended in the beginning of the 1980s, far-left ideologies lost ground. The renewed growth of the 1980s was accompanied by rapid trade and financial liberalization across the globe (Stankov, 2017b). The resulting economic expansions in Western democracies raised labor demand beyond what the local labor markets could fulfill. This spurred an influx of migrants (see Figure 3.6[a] and Figure 3.6[b]), which, in turn, induced an upswing in far-right votes between 1980 and 1990.

Just as the period before the Great Depression was marked by an increasingly vocal far-left, in the early 2000s before the GFC, there was a similar rise. When the good economy of the pre-crisis years resulted in increasing household wealth and shrinking income disparities (see Figure 3.5[b]), the far-left lost its appeal. Figure 3.5(b) offers another insight into the far-left. Similarly to the way immigration leads the far-right, a rise in income disparity precedes a surge in far-left votes. This is particularly visible in the 1980s and around 2000. However, notwithstanding the drifts in income inequality, both ideologies regained traction during the GFC.

The period after the GFC saw a dramatic increase in far-right votes to levels not seen since the Great Depression. A potential explanation is offered in Figure 3.6. The numbers of immigration and asylum-seekers soared after the crisis, imposing significant dissonance costs on local communities and competing for low-skilled jobs with vulnerable native voters. At the same time, far-left votes peaked at about 10% on average, a historical record for far-left parties in modern Western democratic history. Guiso et al. (2017, p. 3) propose an explanation:

> [P]opulist parties are more likely to emerge and prosper when a country has to deal with a crisis of systemic economic security that the traditional incumbent parties […] find hard to address, so that their voters lose faith in them.

Indeed, the post-crisis rise of far-left and far-right parties is concurrent with an overall decline in support for center-left and center parties, consistent with the "tactical extremism" hypothesis for the supply-side of the political

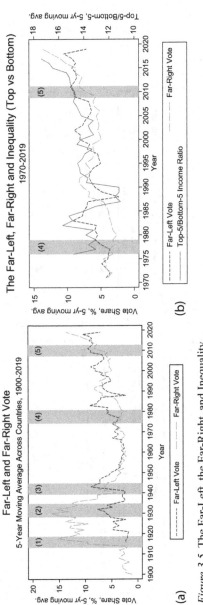

Figure 3.5 The Far-Left, the Far-Right, and Inequality

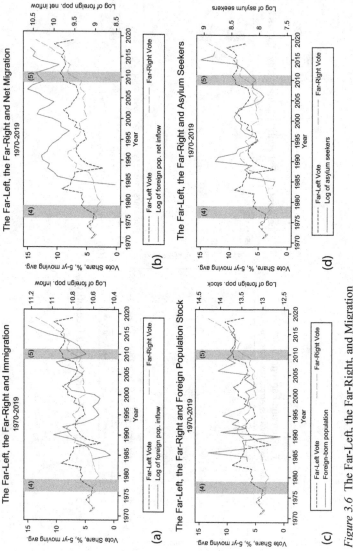

Figure 3.6 The Far-Left, the Far-Right, and Migration

market (Eguia and Giovannoni, 2019). This process, called *center-thinning* – the gradual but steady fade of political support for traditional centrist parties – is presented next.

3.4 The inevitable center-thinning

Centrist ideologies include a wide range of parties scoring between 1.25 and 8.75 on the 0–10 Left–Right scale. This is why separating the trends across center-left, center, and center-right parties is more informative about the direction of voter preferences.

Two trends are worth noticing in the period before WWII, both of which explain voter polarization at the time. First, as the world moved increasingly towards the far-right before the Great Depression, it also experienced a commensurate gradual decline in the vote for center-right parties, from around 45% in the beginning of the century to an average of slightly more than 30% in the depths of the Depression. Most of the decline in center-right parties fed the rise of the far-right.

The rightward polarization, however, is only half the story. The other half is that the large swings in center-left voting before the Depression were moving opposite to the changes in the center. Figure 3.7 illustrates this well. Although less radical, voter polarization to the left was the big political story of the early 20th century. Some of the ground lost by the center was regained in the 1920s, and some of the center-left vote swayed further to the left at the same time. This suggests that voter polarization was an eminent feature of the political landscape before the Great Depression. Center-thinning is also the story of today, underpinned by the eroding representative functions

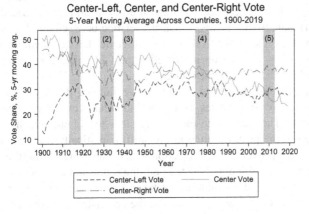

Figure 3.7 Centrist Votes: 1900–2019

of traditional democracies (Kriesi, 2014; Mair, 2002). The reasons for this erosion were discussed in detail in Chapter 2.

When the first democratic elections were held around 1900, a typical centrist party would win a majority with around 50% of the vote, and the second largest group in parliament would typically be the center-right. With a few brief intermissions, this would be the case until approximately the 1970s. The tides turned for the traditional center during the stagflation period. At that time, center-right parties took the central stage, and have dominated the debate ever since. Meanwhile, the traditional center has thinned in favor of the center-right or center-left governments after the GFC.

Since the center-right swept the vote around the mid-1970s with market-oriented reforms, it has been solidifying its positions. Today, it is the strongest wing of the political center. Rising inequality seems not to affect this in any way, as suggested in Figure 3.8. Rather, it is perhaps a result of a historical chance for right-wing parties to dominate the narrative in the late 1970s and early 1980s, to push a number of successes through, and then spread the influence of trade and financial liberalization reforms through supranational institutions after the mid-1980s Latin American balance of payments crises, the early 1990s Eastern European communist collapse, and the emerging markets crisis of 1997–1998. By the early years of the 21st century, as we have seen from the previous chapter, it has been almost taken for granted that market-oriented reforms pushed by the center-left and center-right governments were the only reasonable alternative. That is, until the GFC changed the narrative.

The GFC changed the narrative not only with respect to market-oriented reforms in trade, financial liberalization, and overall deregulation, but also with respect to migration. Figure 3.9 suggests that immigration, in both absolute numbers and in net terms, and asylum-seeking, have a positive relationship with the traditional centrist vote. The correlation was positive at least for the 30 years between 1985 and the European refugee crisis of 2015. It seems that after the refugee crisis the relation between immigration and centrist votes broke down. As the vote for center-left and center-right parties did not change much during or after the GFC, then a reasonable question is: where did the centrist vote go?

A simplistic explanation could be that center-thinning directly contributed to the rise of extreme parties. However, individual voters rarely make dramatic swings. They may vote for a party close to the one which they have preferred in the past, but they rarely shift dramatically from center-right to extreme left over a single election cycle. Therefore, it could be a spillover effect: center-thinning boosted both the center-left and the center-right. However, notice the simultaneous trend-less movement in both of the centrist wings. This means that some of the center-left and center-right voters spilled over to the extreme parties.

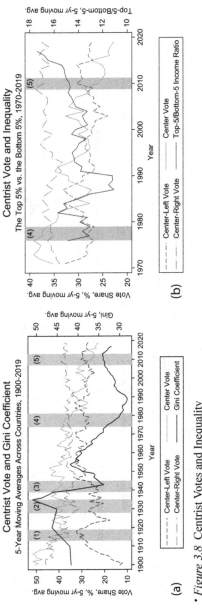

• *Figure 3.8* Centrist Votes and Inequality

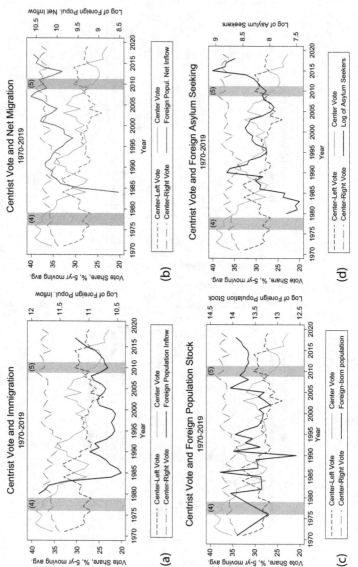

Figure 3.9 Centrist Votes and Migration

Center-thinning is in line with what some call *the centrist paradox* (Adler, 2018). In essence, from an empirical standpoint it is the voters in the center that drive political polarization. The evidence here suggests that this has been the case at least since the 1900s, consistent with recent evidence by Gidron and Ziblatt (2019). However, the data here also implies that when government policies respond to perceived unfairness by providing more adequate social safety nets – as was the case in Western democracies after WWII – then center-thinning is mitigated.

These are hypotheses, which require far more rigorous tests than a mere graphical observation. The observations presented here are more suitable for asking the right questions than for giving the correct answer. Adopting a precise identification strategy for what has driven the seismic changes in the political landscape in the 20th and early 21st century is perhaps an overly ambitious task, as anyone who has worked with country-level panel data studies knows. However, such data can be used for hypothesis testing based on the emerging robust graphical relationships. These hypotheses are presented below.

3.5 Empirical evidence: the *ausmine* triad

Both the theory and the evidence suggest that three empirically tractable factors play major roles in promoting extreme populist votes to the political mainstream: inequality, migration, and austerity. In this section, the hypothesis that all of these factors correlate positively with the dynamics of populist votes is tested. Naturally, there may sometimes be a considerable amount of time between the moment an underlying factor materializes and the moment it actually makes a difference to voter outcomes. Therefore, it makes sense to study how changes in voter outcomes correlate with previous levels of inequality, migration, and austerity. In addition, it is reasonable to believe that those correlations are different at various stages of the business cycle, particularly during booms and recessions. Further, more unequal societies may have different views of migration. Therefore, migration will play a different role in those societies, which calls for the interaction of immigration with inequality in the empirical model used to explain vote share dynamics. The baseline model to test the above hypotheses for the entire panel of countries is as follows:

$$
\begin{aligned}
V_{ict} = \alpha_c + \alpha_t + \alpha_1 V_{ict-1} &+ \beta_1 In_{ct-1} + \beta_2 Imm_{ct-1} + \beta_3 G_{ct-1} \\
&+ \beta_4 \left(y * In \right)_{ct-1} + \beta_5 \left(y * Imm \right)_{ct-1} + \beta_6 \left(y * G \right)_{ct-1} \\
&+ \beta_7 \left(Imm * In \right)_{ct-1} + \varepsilon_{ict},
\end{aligned}
\tag{3.1}
$$

where V_{ict} is the change of the vote share for ideology i in country c in election period t; α_c and α_t are country and time-fixed effects, respectively; V_{ict-1} is the share of votes for ideology i at the previous elections; In_{ct-1} is the measure of inequality (the Gini coefficient); Imm_{ct-1} is the natural logarithm of the inflow of foreign-born population; G_{ct-1} is the natural logarithm of government expenditures in country c in election period $t-1$; $(y*In)_{ct-1}$, $(y*Imm)_{ct-1}$, $(y*G)_{ct-1}$ are the interaction effects of GDP per capita (y) with inequality, immigration, and government expenditures, respectively; $(Imm* In)_{ct-1}$ is the interaction effect of immigration and inequality; and ε_{ict} is the part of the vote share for ideology i left unexplained by the model. Standard errors within a country over time are naturally not independent of each other. Therefore, they are assumed to be correlated, which implies those standard errors need to be clustered at the country level for a robust estimation to take place.

The results in Table 3.2 demonstrate a variety of ways in which immigration, inequality, and austerity correlate with changes in voter outcomes across countries over time. Before analyzing those correlations, however, the inherent vote share dynamics are worth noting. Even in the absence of any underlying drivers, there will be a natural vote share cycle. A higher outcome in previous elections typically results in a slightly lower outcome in current elections, and vice versa. This result is valid for any party affiliation, as the parameter estimates for $Vote_{t-1}$ are highly significant. Just as the business cycle oscillates around a certain long-term trend, the political cycle has its own short-term cycles within the three massive waves. The graphical evidence supported this inherent political cycle hypothesis and it now emerges in the regression estimates as well.

Whereas the inherent political cycle is evident for all ideologies and party groups, the alleged impact of inequality on their vote share is different. Unlike previous evidence in Stankov (2017a) and Stankov (2018), higher inequality is typically correlated with increased support for far-left parties, but not for far-right ones. The simultaneous slump in center-left votes suggests voter polarization to the left at higher levels of income inequality. There is some additional evidence that higher income inequality also triggers a right-wing shift of preferences. However, the right-wing polarization does not go through the same cycle as the left-wing: far-right votes seem unaffected by inequality.

There are other powerful triggers of far-right votes. Austerity – reductions of government expenditures – is one of them. Austerity seemingly has a profound effect on the vote shares of both far-right and far-left parties. This has also been shown using within-country and individual-level data (Alabrese et al., 2019; Becker et al., 2017; Fetzer, 2019). Unlike extreme

Table 3.2 Vote Share Dynamics: Panel Data Estimates

	(1) ΔFar-Left$_t$	(2) ΔFar-Right$_t$	(3) ΔTEV$_t$	(4) ΔCen-Left$_t$	(5) ΔCen$_t$	(6) ΔCen-Right$_t$
Vote$_{t-1}$	-0.860***	-0.667***	-0.664***	-1.068***	-0.648***	-0.604***
	(0.187)	(0.167)	(0.168)	(0.187)	(0.111)	(0.223)
Gini	62.944***	-9.932	-0.263	-16.171**	-5.995	13.984**
	(14.151)	(7.431)	(10.780)	(6.867)	(8.398)	(6.168)
Immigr	-121.296***	16.566	-3.559	50.602***	26.053	-50.883***
	(25.375)	(16.130)	(30.360)	(17.743)	(23.222)	(17.016)
Gov.exp.	-102.259***	-29.211***	-30.562***	5.488	3.550	7.032
	(23.989)	(10.881)	(10.689)	(7.064)	(11.192)	(11.751)
GDPc*In	-5.569***	0.609	-0.304	1.558**	0.771	-1.516**
	(1.143)	(0.766)	(1.154)	(0.690)	(0.913)	(0.605)
GDPc*Imm	12.853***	-2.795*	-0.682	-5.021***	-1.799	4.420***
	(2.903)	(1.515)	(2.771)	(1.649)	(2.154)	(1.624)
GDPc*G	4.785***	1.892**	1.962**	-0.024	-0.581	-0.129
	(1.266)	(0.914)	(0.816)	(0.731)	(0.829)	(0.722)
Ineq*Imm	-0.385*	0.316*	0.291*	0.017	-0.212	0.186
	(0.225)	(0.173)	(0.157)	(0.143)	(0.219)	(0.159)
Obs.	45	124	136	168	168	167
R²-within	0.995	0.569	0.525	0.673	0.521	0.499

Notes: The estimated model is Equation (3.1), as detailed in the text. Vote$_{t-1}$ is the vote share of the respective party group on the previous elections. Gini is the lagged value of the Gini coefficient. Immigr is the lagged natural logarithm of foreign population inflow. Gov.exp. is the lagged natural logarithm of government expenditures. The rest are interaction terms of GDP per capita with inequality, immigration, and government expenditures (GDPc*), and of inequality with immigration, as detailed in the text. The model includes country and time fixed effects. Standard errors are clustered on country level and are in parentheses. Symbols: * $p < .10$, ** $p < .05$, *** $p < .01$.

left and extreme right votes, center-left, center, and center-right groups appear impervious to the dynamics of government expenditures. This is not the case with immigration.

Immigration allegedly moves votes from the center-right to the center-left. Countries with larger immigration flows are also more prone to vote center-left. To some extent, this is expected, as immigration typically flows to countries with more generous social systems in the first place. If those countries traditionally vote for center-left governments, then we will observe a positive association between immigration and center-left votes, even in the absence of a causal relationship between the two. In addition, we observe smaller immigration flows to countries governed by center-right governments. As these countries often have more restrictive immigration systems, a negative association is also easily predictable.

What is less predictable is how votes depend on *in*equality, *m*igration, and *aus*terity – the "*ausmine*" triad, for devotees of neologisms – along the business cycle. The answer to this question is given by the parameter estimates on the interaction terms of GDP per capita and those *ausmine* factors in Table 3.2: $GDPc*In$, $GDPc*Imm$, and $GDPc*G$, respectively. The Table suggests that voters become more sensitive to changes in inequality during recessions, which are also typically accompanied by a downturn in per capita GDP. The negative coefficient for far-left votes indicates that a downturn in income per capita raises the popularity of the extreme left. Again, this may occur at the expense of center-left votes, signaled by the significant and positive parameter estimates of $GDPc*In$. If the coefficient is positive, then an income per capita recession drives center-left votes down.

Similarly to what we have observed with the baseline inequality effect, a rise in inequality during a recession is also associated with a shift to the center-right. Just as above, however, the positive correlation may be due to the fact that center-right governments typically cope with recessions by lowering taxes. As this favors the rich more than the poor, inequality increases. As a result, using the methods above may not allow us to distinguish between the true impact of inequality on votes during recessions, and the counter-cyclical effect from center-right policy choices into inequality.

A similar reverse causality may plague the interpretation of the other recessionary interactions with austerity and immigration. This, however, does not make them less interesting. During recessions, the far-right vote becomes more responsive to immigration, extending what Hatton (2016) finds for a sample of 20 European countries. This is implied by the negative and significant interaction term of $GDPc*Imm$. As the far-right rises, the center-right fades after recessions in countries with larger inflows of immigrants. This is a similar polarization effect to that observed for inequality at the other end of the political spectrum. It seems that far-left and far-right polarization are two different phenomena driven by inequality and migration, respectively. The correlation of those factors with extreme votes becomes more pronounced during recessions.

Unlike inequality and immigration which affect extreme left and extreme right votes differently, austerity triggers comparable discontent in both far-left and far-right votes, particularly during recessions. This is exposed in the positive parameter estimates on the $GDPc*G$ interaction term. An austerity measure will have a larger impact on extreme votes in an economy which is already stagnating or in outright recession. Similarly to the baseline effect of government expenditures, austerity does not affect the center-left, center, or center-right votes differently along the business cycle. The same is true for the joint significance of inequality and migration.

Although the centrist vote seems unaffected by the joint impact of inequality and migration, the extreme vote is responsive to it. Societies experiencing higher immigration are more likely to vote far-right if inequality is also high. This is seen from the parameter estimates on the $Ineq*Imm$ interaction term, and fits the model predictions by Besley and Persson (2019), Collier (2019), and Pastor and Veronesi (2018), among others. At the same time, a boost for the far-left is expected in societies with low inequality and low initial levels of immigration.

The last result, like most of the results for the far-left parties, should be approached with caution. The number of observations is too small, and the fit of the model within panels is suspiciously high. This implies the model might be mis-specified, or that outliers drive the results, among other identification issues. Also note that the results above are based on a model which is far from exhaustive. There are omitted variable biases in the estimates for each ideology i. The most obvious omitted variables – the common time shocks across countries (i.e., time fixed effects), and the unobserved drivers of the vote at the country level, which remain constant over time (i.e., country fixed effects) – were included in the model. Their inclusion is dictated by the influential results of Arzheimer and Carter (2006), who find both fixed and variable country-level effects to be significant for explaining extreme right votes.

However, other factors suggested in Chapter 2 are also difficult to observe and measure and vary over time. Among them are leader charisma and endogenous voter identity, which can play decisive roles in determining voter outcomes in some countries, and insignificant roles in others. The size and significance of the effect will depend on the importance voters choose to place on those particular unobservable time-varying issues relative to their economic situation.

Ideally, one would like to control for those unobservable time-varying factors at the country level by saturating the model with a full set of interactions of year and country dummies. Yet, in a country-level panel data environment, this is often an unaffordable luxury, as the data for many country-years and many explanatory variables is still scarce, especially before the 1960s. One way to get around this limitation is to artificially inflate the number of observations by assuming voter outcomes are constant *within* electoral cycles. Funke et al. (2016) adopted this strategy to explore post-crisis voter polarization. However, even though mismeasurement of the dependent variable does not lead to inconsistent estimates, this strategy cannot uncover the impact of all relevant explanatory factors at the country level.

An additional way to expose those unobservable country-level factors is to resort to the classic case study methodology often adopted in the study of populism at the cost of losing the big picture. This approach has led to valuable contributions in explaining Latin American populism (Dornbusch and Edwards, 1990; Kaufman and Stallings, 1991; Lago, 1991), European populism (Cahill, 2007; Mudde and Rovira Kaltwasser, 2011; Učeň, 2007) and East-Asian nationalism (Hewison, 2005; Tejapira, 2002). As revealing as it may be, the case study approach comes at a significant cost: it misses the common underlying factors of political dynamics across countries. This chapter focused on some of those, and in particular, on austerity, migration, and income inequality.

Even though austerity, migration, and inequality have some power to explain the dynamics of both populist and non-populist votes over long periods of time, and particularly during recessions, they are far from being the only influencers of those dynamics. Future empirical studies from economics, political science, and sociology will show more rigor than the above model in identifying the causal mechanisms behind extreme vote changes. As the works of Margalit (2019a) and Margalit (2019b) show, the debates in both political science and economics are still very much open.

A promising way to advance the debates is to tackle the measurement of endogenous voter identity on an individual level, and interact it with the socio-economic factors we have discussed here in empirical models of extreme votes. An additional avenue for research is to empirically delve into the impact of austerity, immigration, and inequality on extreme votes along the skill distribution. A further extension is to gradually uncover the impact of the unobservable effects by collecting more data in the spirit of Arzheimer and Carter (2006). Finally, whatever the models used, their causal interpretation demands a far more carefully crafted identification strategy than that applied here. To be able to design such strategies, researchers will need to rely on more extensive data coverage. Ideally, larger within-country data availability of migrant inflows, trade exposure, and inequalities is the place to start. The data exist for some countries but not for most, and this is why empirical studies of populist votes will perhaps focus on country-level analyses, at least for now. With the current cross-country panel data availability, this is as far as this type of analysis can currently go.

Bibliography

Adler, D. (2018). The centrist paradox. Working Paper, Social Science Research Network. Mimeo.

Alabrese, E., Becker, S. O., Fetzer, T., & Novy, D. (2019). Who voted for Brexit? Individual and regional data combined. *European Journal of Political Economy*, *56*, 132–150.

Arzheimer, K., & Carter, E. (2006). Political opportunity structures and right-wing extremist party success. *European Journal of Political Research*, *45*(3), 419–443.

Bakker, R., de Vries, C., Edwards, E., Hooghe, L., Jolly, S., Marks, G., & Vachudova, M. A. (2015). Measuring party positions in Europe: The chapel hill expert survey trend file, 1999–2010. *Party Politics*, *21*(1), 143–152.

Becker, S. O., Fetzer, T., & Novy, D. (2017). Who voted for Brexit? A comprehensive district-level analysis. *Economic Policy*, *32*(92), 601–650.

Benoit, K., & Laver, M. (2006). *Party policy in modern democracies*. Routledge Research in Comparative Politics. Routledge.

Besley, T., & Persson, T. (2019). The rise of identity politics. Working Paper, London School of Economics.

Bolt, J., Inklaar, R., de Jong, H., & van Zanden, J. L. (2018). Maddison project database, version 2018. Rebasing 'Maddison': New income comparisons and the shape of long-run economic development. Working Paper 10, Maddison Project.

Cachanosky, N., & Padilla, A. (2019). A panel data analysis of Latin American populism. Technical Report, Metropolitan State University of Denver, Economics Department. Mimeo.

Cahill, B. (2007). Of note: Institutions, populism, and immigration in Europe. *SAIS Review*, *27*(1), 79–80.

Castles, F. G., & Mair, P. (1984). Left-right political scales: Some 'expert' judgments. *European Journal of Political Research*, *12*(1), 73–88.

Collier, P. (2019). Diverging identities: A model of class formation. Working Paper SM-WP-2019-01, Blavatnik School of Government, University of Oxford.

Döring, H., & Manow, P. (2019). Parliaments and governments database (parlgov): Information on parties, elections and cabinets in modern democracies. Accessed September 29, 2019 from http://www.parlgov.org/

Dornbusch, R., & Edwards, S. (1990). Macroeconomic populism. *Journal of Development Economics*, *32*(2), 247–277.

Eguia, J. X., & Giovannoni, F. (2019). Tactical extremism. *American Political Science Review*, *113*(1), 282–286.

Fetzer, T. (2019). Did austerity cause Brexit? *American Economic Review*, *109*(11), 3849–3886.

Funke, M., Schularick, M., & Trebesch, C. (2016). Going to extremes: Politics after financial crises, 1870–2014. *European Economic Review*, *88*, 227–260.

Gidron, N., & Ziblatt, D. (2019). Center-right political parties in advanced democracies. *Annual Review of Political Science, 22*(1), 17–35.

Guiso, L., Herrera, H., Morelli, M., & Sonno, T. (2017). Populism: Demand and supply. Discussion Papers Series 11871, Centre for Economic Policy Research.

Hatton, T. J. (2016). Immigration, public opinion and the recession in Europe. *Economic Policy, 31*(86), 205–246.

Heinö, A. J. (2019). *Timbro authoritarian populism Index 2019.* Timbro Institute, Stockholm, Sweden.

Hewison, K. (2005). Neo-liberalism and domestic capital: The political outcomes of the economic crisis in Thailand. *The Journal of Development Studies, 41*(2), 310–330.

Hopkin, J., & Blyth, M. (2019). The global economics of European populism: Growth regimes and party system change in Europe (the *Government and Opposition/* Leonard Schapiro lecture 2017). *Government and Opposition, 54*(2), 193–225.

Huber, J., & Inglehart, R. (1995). Expert interpretations of party space and party locations in 42 societies. *Party Politics, 1*(1), 73–111.

Jordà, O., Schularick, M., & Taylor, A. M. (2017). Macrofinancial history and the new business cycle facts. In M. Eichenbaum and J. A. Parker (Eds.), *NBER Macroeconomics Annual 2016, Volume 31* (pp. 213–263). University of Chicago Press.

Kaufman, R. R., & Stallings, B. (1991). The political economy of Latin American populism. In R. Dornbusch & S. Edwards (Eds.), *The macroeconomics of populism in Latin America* (pp. 15–43). University of Chicago Press.

Kriesi, H. (2014). The populist challenge. *Western European Politics, 37*(2), 361–378.

Lago, R. (1991). The illusion of pursuing redistribution through macropolicy: Peru's heterodox experience, 1985–1990. In R. Dornbusch & S. Edwards (Eds.), *The macroeconomics of populism in Latin America* (pp. 263–330). University of Chicago Press.

Mair, P. (2002). Populist democracy vs party democracy. In Y. Mény & Y. Surel (Eds.), *Democracies and the populist challenge* (pp. 81–98). London: Palgrave Macmillan UK.

Margalit, Y. (2019a). Economic insecurity and the causes of populism, reconsidered. *Journal of Economic Perspectives, 33*(4), 152–170.

Margalit, Y. (2019b). Political responses to economic shocks. *Annual Review of Political Science, 22*(1), 277–295.

Milanovic, B. L. (2014). All the Ginis, 1950–2012. Updated in Autumn 2014. World Bank, Washington, DC.

Mudde, C., & Rovira Kaltwasser, C. (2011). Voices of the peoples: Populism in Europe and Latin America compared. Technical Report, Kellog Institute for International Studies.

Norris, P., & Inglehart, R. (2019). *Cultural backlash and the rise of populism: Trump, Brexit, and authoritarian populism.* Cambridge University Press.

OECD. (2019). International migration database. Retrieved October 5, 2019 from https://stats.oecd.org/

Pastor, L., & Veronesi, P. (2018). Inequality aversion, populism, and the backlash against globalization. Working Paper 24900, National Bureau of Economic Research.

Rode, M., & Revuelta, J. (2015). The wild bunch! An empirical note on populism and economic institutions. *Economics of Governance 16*(1), 73–96.

Stankov, P. (2017a). Crises, welfare, and populism. In *Economic freedom and welfare before and after the crisis* (pp. 135–164). Cham: Springer International Publishing.

Stankov, P. (2017b). Policies and reforms. In *Economic freedom and welfare before and after the crisis* (pp. 43–67). Cham: Springer International Publishing.

Stankov, P. (2018). The political economy of populism: An empirical investigation. *Comparative Economic Studies, 60*(2), 230–253.

Tejapira, K. (2002). Post-crisis economic impasse and political recovery in Thailand: The resurgence of economic nationalism. *Critical Asian Studies, 34*(3), 323–356.

Učeň, P. (2007). Parties, populism, and anti-establishment politics in East Central Europe. *SAIS Review, 27*(1), 49–62.

United Nations. (2019). World population prospects: The 2019 revision. Retrieved October 15, 2019 from https://population.un.org/

UNU-WIDER. (2018). World income inequality database (WIID4.0). UNU-WIDER, Helsinki, Finland. Downloaded September 13, 2019 from https://www.wider.unu.edu/data/

WID.World. (2019). The world inequality database. Retrieved October 5, 2019 from https://wid.world/

4 The political and economic consequences of populism

Chapter 3 has shown what delivers power to populists. This chapter discusses what they do once they assume power from two perspectives: the impact of populist governments on the state of democracy, and the corresponding effect on the economy.

4.1 What do populists do?

It would be overly simplistic to think about cycles of populism as cycles of election outcomes alone. Election outcomes are a function of the underlying dynamics of identity and the economy, and election outcomes also predict the future democratic development. There have been enough populists in power, including in Europe and the OECD. Based on their record of policies, we are able to draw some conclusions about what populists do, and whether populism retains the progressive and corrective functions that were outlined in the introductory chapter after its representatives assume power. Analyses of populist *modus operandi* in both political and economic spheres have been numerous, but they have been predominantly based on case studies. The quantitative literature of populist methods is still in its nascent stages.

Taggart and Rovira Kaltwasser (2016) summarize the case study approach. The approach centers on the ways in which key traits of populist parties and leaders change from the moment they attain power. This turning point is important because it usually marks their transition from the political fringe to the mainstream. Once in power, several factors play a role in how populists operate.

The operational strategies of populists are limited by the existing constitutional structure, especially the separation of powers. Their operational strategies are also limited by whether they have been elected as the leading party with a ruling majority or as a junior coalition member (Taggart and Rovira Kaltwasser, 2016, p. 358). When a populist is elected to an office with considerable powers, pre-emptive disruption of the effectiveness of the opposition is a typical political strategy. The opposition is seen not only in the nearest rival political parties but also in the autonomous judiciary (Brewer-Carías, 2010; Colburn, 2011) and in civil society organizations of local and international origins, as well as independent media, including social networks (Denisova, 2017). This is done to prolong the populists' political longevity, typically early in their tenure in office to maximize the effectiveness of the pre-emptive strategy, while the opposition is still re-grouping after their electoral loss.

de la Torre and Lemos (2016, p. 221) argue that a key element of this strategy is capturing the judiciary. Once the judiciary is under control, representatives of civil society and independent media can no longer use legal mechanisms to resist the "crack down on civil society and the regulation of private media." These strategies have been seen both in Latin America and in Europe. Notable recent European incidences of populist backlash against accountability include Hungary (Batory, 2016), Poland (Matthes, 2016), the Czech Republic (Pehe, 2018), and especially Russia (Evans, 2011; Sakwa, 2011). By amending the government structure and the fabric of civil society, populists in power undermine democracy. This is seen particularly strongly in times of rising commodity prices, which soften government budget constraints, thereby reducing the costs of obtaining and retaining political rents.

Significant limitations on those rents, however, are in place when populists have managed to break through the electoral sieve into parliament, but are acting as junior partners in a government formed by a mainstream party. In such cases, democratic erosion may not occur (Taggart and Rovira Kaltwasser, 2016, p. 358), although government priorities may shift toward producing either economic or identity rents for the populist voters. In turn, heeding those rents and adjusting policies with them in mind may re-enfranchise significant portions of the electorate which had previously become disconnected from the political mainstream. Thus, when applied in small doses, populist incumbency can serve as a corrective to mainstream party policies, which usually favor the rents of the ruling elite and their constituencies. This is in stark contrast with the above-mentioned dire political consequences of a populist with a ruling majority.

In a recent work, Kendall-Taylor et al. (2019, p. 3) summarize the political consequences of a dominant populist incumbency. Populists typically assume power through a democratic process. Once in power, they pursue policies which undermine democracy in small increments. Their strategy is to "leverage societal dissatisfaction to gradually undercut institutional constraints on their own rule, sideline opponents, and weaken civil society." This strategy for eroding democracy is nearly identical in most contemporary episodes of populist rule. But the playbook is quite old. The same approach was used by far-left and far-right dictatorships alike in 1920s and 1930s Germany, Italy, and Soviet Russia, by Latin American populists in the 1950s and 1960s, by military regimes in the 1970s, and by the modern-day populists in Latin America before the GFC. An identical strategy is applied by virtually all European populists in power today.

The perilous actions of incumbent populists in the political domain are in tandem with similarly disruptive, and in most cases detrimental, consequences for the economy. Since the works of Dornbusch and Edwards (1990) and Dornbusch and Edwards (1991a), we have a clear overview of those consequences. Using a case study approach, Dornbusch and Edwards (1990, p. 247) demonstrate that "macroeconomic populism is an approach to economics that emphasizes growth and income distribution and deemphasizes the risks of inflation and deficit finance, external constraints and the reaction of economic agents to aggressive non-market policies." Despite the different political environments leading to populist incumbencies, the authors demonstrate that the populist approach to macroeconomic policies ultimately leads to economic distress and crises. When crises do occur as a result of populist policies, "it is always at a frightening cost to the very groups who were supposed to be favored" (p. 247).

The approaches taken to macroeconomic policy-making under populist governance have featured so many common characteristics that it is fair to call it *the populist paradigm* (Dornbusch and Edwards, 1991a) or *the populist playbook* (Dalio et al., 2017). The populist playbook includes protectionism, nationalism, increased infrastructure-building, increased military spending, greater budget deficits, and capital controls (Dalio et al., 2017, p. 2).

Rode and Revuelta (2015) detail the consequences for macroeconomic policies. Using a sample of 33 developed and developing countries, they find that populist governments "erode legal security, reduce freedom to trade, and tighten economic regulation" (p. 73). Early evidence on the macroeconomic consequences of populist governance went beyond legal security and anti-globalization policies. Dornbusch and Edwards (1990, p. 248) demonstrated that overly expansionary fiscal policies have inevitably led to uncontrollable inflation, exchange rate and banking crises, recessions, and real wage cuts.

Why do these detrimental policies make political sense, at least *ex-ante*, and why do voters fall for them? Dovis et al. (2016) study the motives of governments for embarking on overly expansionary debt trajectories. Motivated by high levels of income inequality, an incumbent government will run fiscal deficits and institute redistribution policies of generous social welfare and compensation packages. Initially, the economy booms, but the boom is accompanied by excessive current account deficits. Those current account deficits lead to currency crises, and rapid readjustment of redistribution and spending policies. In other words, they lead to greater inequality and lower welfare transfers, effectively imposing austerity measures on an economy which has previously borrowed excessively. Ultimately, voters who elected the populist government end up worse off.

Voters may fall for those policy proposals because they are living in a *fiscal illusion* (Alesina and Passalacqua, 2015; Buchanan and Wagner, 1977): When they anticipate government spending increases or tax reductions, they reward the incumbent governments and ignore the longer-term consequences on debt. It is easy to see the potential for political gain from this blissful illusion, and politicians readily offer it, often even those to the right of the center (Acemoglu et al., 2013). As a result, governments apply fiscal policies biased towards deficit spending, especially before elections. Alesina and Passalacqua (2015) discuss the occurrence of deficit biases among developed economies. As those biases in Latin America are particularly strong, the mismatch between the current debt and the optimal debt level run by a benevolent social planner will be larger in those economies. The mismatch leads to a higher likelihood of macroeconomic crises, wage cuts, hyperinflation episodes (Saboin-Garcia, 2018), and inequality hikes often seen in Latin America in the aftermath of populist governments.

Depending on the local context, depressing voter welfare may lead to populism fatigue and thus lessen populist votes in future elections, as found earlier by Stankov (2017) and Stankov (2018). However, it can also sharpen the salience of underlying conditions that led to a populist incumbency (Mian et al., 2014), especially in environments of high income inequality, rising immigration, and austerity (see Chapters 2 and 3).

In what follows, I examine the political consequences of populist governments from an empirical standpoint, and review recent evidence on the correlation of populist incumbencies on key macroeconomic indicators. The data for exploring those correlations is presented below, followed by the estimation models and the results.

4.2 Data

The *Cabinet* sheet in the Döring and Manow (2019) dataset features the far-left and far-right parties that succeeded in entering a parliament in 33 parliamentary democracies since 1903. Those democracies include all of today's European Union countries after their democratic transition, as well as the OECD countries which are not presidential systems. Most are developed countries, and a full list appears in Table 3.1. Döring and Manow (2019) include national lower house chamber elections since 1900 and the

European Parliamentary (EP) elections since 1979. To allow comparability across countries, electoral outcomes on EP elections have been omitted.

The Döring and Manow (2019) data contains information on 11,007 electoral outcomes of parties in the 33 democracies. For 9,805 of the electoral outcomes, the data records the party's ideological position on the Left–Right scale, which identifies extreme left and extreme right parties. The ideological position in the Döring and Manow (2019) data is a simple average of the party positions in four earlier studies of party positions and spaces: Castles and Mair (1984), Huber and Inglehart (1995), Benoit and Laver (2006), and Bakker et al. (2015). Importantly, the data can reveal the amount of influence each of those parties wielded in the post-election governments: e.g. if they were part of the ruling government, or not; the number of seats each party won in the lower house; and whether the prime minister after each election belonged to a far-left or a far-right party.

The data on those electoral outcomes demonstrates that far-left and far-right parties were a part of the political fringes for most of the modern democratic history of their respective countries. However, in some cases, those parties had sufficient political clout to support a government, and in rare instances led to the election of extreme left or extreme right prime ministers. Table 4.1 summarizes the number of occasions in which extreme parties managed to become part of a government, and in which they nominated a prime minister.

In Panel A, a more restrictive definition of "extreme party" is applied, in line with the traditional definition in Castles and Mair (1984, p. 87). This

Table 4.1 Cabinets with Far-Left or Far-Right Parties

	Cabinet w/ Far Left	Cabinet w/ Far Right	PM: Far Left	PM: Far Right
	Panel A: Left–Right index below 1.25 or above 8.75			
Total	470	211	470	211
0	439	200	464	211
1	31	11	6	0
	Panel B: Left–Right index below 1.50 or above 8.50			
Total	558	377	558	377
0	515	277	552	350
1	43	100	6	27

Notes: the table shows the total number of national elections in which a populist party entered parliament in the Döring and Manow (2019) data. Two definitions of populist parties are explored. In Panel A (B), a party is defined as left-wing populist if the Döring and Manow (2019) Left–Right index is below 1.25 (1.50); and right-wing populist if the Left–Right index is above 8.75 (8.50). Within those elections, the table shows the number of coalition cabinets formed with the help of a far-left or far-right party (Cabinet with Far Left = 1, Cabinet with Far Right = 1); and the number of elections which led to a far-left or a far-right prime minister (PM: Far Left = 1, PM: Far Right = 1).

designates a party as far-left if its position on the Left–Right scale is below 1.25, and far-right if its position is above 8.75. However, this restrictive definition of an extreme party does not allow observations of any far-right prime ministers. A slightly more inclusive definition of the extreme – with the thresholds moved to 1.50 and 8.50, respectively – leads to a significant increase in the number of cabinets formed with the help of a far-left or a far-right party, as well as the emergence of some far-right prime ministers. The numbers of cabinets and prime ministers as a result of this modification are presented in Panel B. The political and economic consequences of populist incumbency are studied using the data in Panel B.

The political consequences of populist incumbency can be measured in two broad ways. First, we can compare the existing indices of *Political Rights* (PR) and *Civil Liberties* (CL) in countries governed by populists and in countries run by moderate politicians. The *Freedom in the World* survey produced by Freedom House (2018) contains those indices. The Freedom House (2018) data contains 9,635 observations on political rights and civil liberties in 205 countries and territories since 1972. The political rights index includes components related to the electoral process, political pluralism, and the functioning of government, while the civil rights index measures freedom of expression, freedom to organize, the rule of law, and personal autonomy. A given country or territory is assigned an index of 1 if it experiences the greatest degree of political or civil freedom, and an index of 7 if it has the smallest degree of freedom.

A synthetic overall index of democratic status is then assigned to each country-year based on the average of the *Political Rights* and *Civil Liberties* indices. This average is coded into an overall freedom status rating of *Free*, *Partially Free*, or *Not Free*. For the purposes of our analysis, the scores are translated into numbers as follows: *Free* countries are given a numerical score of 1, *Partially Free* countries are assigned a score of 2, and *Not Free* countries are coded at an overall numerical status (NS) of 3.[1] The match between the populist incumbents from the Döring and Manow (2019) and the *Freedom in the World* data is on 1,504 country-year observations.

Second, in addition to the Freedom House (2018) data, key insights into how populist governments correlate with democratic parameters can be studied using the Marshall et al. (2019) data. The data contains 17,562 observations of political regime characteristics in 193 countries and territories since the year 1800. The political regime characteristics are coded along several dimensions of authority. The coding leads to three synthetic measures: *Democracy (Dem)*, *Autocracy (Aut)*, and an overall *Polity-2 (P-2)* index. The overall *Dem* index varies from 0–10, with the more developed democracies scoring higher; the overall *Aut* index varies from 0–10, with more developed autocracies scoring higher. The *P-2* index is the difference between *Dem* and *Aut* indices, and therefore ranges between −10 and 10. Marshall et al. (2019, pp. 14–16) provides a full description of how the indices are constructed.

Both the Freedom House (2018) and the Marshall et al. (2019) datasets can uncover the impact of populist governance on various political characteristics. However, the impact of populist policies cannot be fully analyzed without studying the effects of their economic policies. Such studies have been pioneered by Dornbusch and Edwards (1990) and Dornbusch and Edwards (1991b), who use case studies of macroeconomic policy-making in Latin American countries. In what follows, their analysis is expanded with more recent macro data indicating the real, monetary, and fiscal consequences in the 33 democracies either governed by populists or with involvement of populist parties in government.

The Jordà et al. (2017) data is rich in historical macro-financial variables which potentially correlate with populist rule. Four distinct groups of economic consequences can be traced back to populism. Those include the following macro-variables:

1. Real dynamics: log of real GDP per capita in PPP prices (*RGDPcP*), real GDP per capita index (*RGDPc*), real consumption per capita index (*Cons*), investment to GDP ratio (*I/Y*), and the logs of nominal import (*Imp*) and export (*Exp*);
2. Monetary indicators: narrow money (*N-Money*), broad money (*B-Money*), short-term nominal interest rates (*STNIR*), and long-term nominal interest rates (*LTNIR*);
3. Fiscal stance: public debt to GDP ratio (*D/GDP*), log of nominal government revenues (*GRev*), log of nominal government expenditures (*GExp*), local currency exchange rate with the USD: Local/USD (*XRate*), and a dummy variable indicating a systemic financial crisis (*Crisis*);
4. Access to finance: log of total nominal loans to the non-financial private sector in local currency (*TLoans*), log of total nominal mortgage loans to the non-financial private sector in local currency (*TMort*), log of total nominal loans to the household sector in local currency (*THH*), log of total nominal business loans in local currency (*TBus*), and the index of nominal house prices (*HPrice*).

Models that enable an understanding of the dynamics of democracy and the economy under populist rule are presented below. The access to finance indicators are a fruitful ground for a separate study, which is why the economic consequences are studied with the help of the three sets of indicators in Jordà et al. (2017).

4.3 Models

The debate on how to analyze incumbent government behavior with economic methods was initiated by the work of Downs (1957), among others. The models discussed here are by no means exhaustive and are only a first step towards a strategy for identifying the causal impact of populist rule on political and economic phenomena. Until their causal impact is identified, the estimates from the models should be treated as populist *correlates* rather than populist consequences. Still, the models are constructed so that the estimates are informative of the potential economic and political consequences of populist governance.

The political consequences of populism are studied using two versions of the following model:

$$D_{mct} = \alpha_c + \alpha_t + \alpha_1 D_{mct-1} + \beta_i \sum_{i=0}^{4} PM_{ct-i} + \beta_j \sum_{j=0}^{4} Cabinet_{ct-j}$$
$$+ \beta_k \sum_{k=0}^{4} CabSeat_{ct-k} + \varepsilon_{mct}, \tag{4.1}$$

where D_{mct} is a democracy measure m in country c in time t; α_c and α_t are country and time fixed effects, respectively; D_{mct-1} is the level of the democracy measure m in period $t-1$; $PM_{ct} = 1$ if the prime-minister has been elected from a far-left or far-right party; $Cabinet_{ct} = 1$ if the cabinet contains far-left or far-right parties; $CabSeat_{ct}$ is the interaction of the $Cabinet_{ct}$ dummy with the share of parliamentary seats occupied by a far-left or far-right party; and ε_{mct} is an error term. The model is estimated separately for far-left and far-right parties. Standard errors are clustered at the country level.

The lagged-dependent level of populism is necessary because populism exhibits long historical roots. Once a given country adopts a populist stance, it is hard to change it in the short-term. For example, Ochsner and Rösel (2016) demonstrate that far-right parties today have significantly stronger voter appeal in regions that accepted more migration from escaping Nazis after WWII. The mechanism of impact is the following: Nazis joined or themselves founded far-right organizations, which have preserved their ideologies over time. Stankov (2018) also exposed the significance of the lagged levels of the dependent variables in the study of populism.

The democracy measures m are different in the two main datasets of dependent variables. In the Freedom House (2018) data, the three dependent variables are *Political Rights* (*PR*), *Civil Liberties* (*CL*), and *Numerical Status* (*NS*). *NS* is the numerical equivalent of the original Freedom House (2018) Status index, with the following translation into numerical values:

Free (F)=1, Partially Free (PF)=2, and Not Free (NF)=3. Note that more developed democracies are given *lower* indices in the Freedom House (2018) data.

Initially, a limited version of the model is estimated to demonstrate how cabinets including far-left or far-right parties correlate with various measures of democracy. Thus, Equation (4.1) simplifies to:

$$D_{mct} = \alpha_c + \alpha_t + \alpha_1 D_{mct-1} + \beta_j \sum_{j=0}^{4} Cabinet_{ct-j} + \varepsilon_{mct}, \qquad (4.2)$$

where the reading of variables is identical to those in Equation (4.1). As the simplified model omits relevant variables, the full version is estimated next. The usefulness of separating the estimations for *Cabinets* and *Prime Ministers* is to see whether incumbent populists have a different correlation with measures of democracy when they serve as junior coalition members than in the periods in which they from a government. The tables with results specify which equation has been used.

The estimated models for *Cabinets* and *Prime Ministers* are repeated with the Marshall et al. (2019) data, where the dependent variables are the level of *Democracy* (*Dem*), the level of *Autocracy* (*Aut*), and an all-encompassing *Polity-2* (*P-2*) index. Separating democratic and autocratic patterns of authority is necessary, given the proliferation of democratic regimes after the Global Financial Crisis (Bogaards, 2009; Cianetti et al., 2018). The results from estimating the above models with the Marshall et al. (2019) data are reported separately from the estimates based on Freedom House (2018) data. Note that more developed democracies are given *higher* indices in the Marshall et al. (2019) data, so the interpretation of identical parameter estimates across the two datasets will be different.

The models used to measure the economic consequences of populist governance are similar to those used for the political consequences. As before, both limited and full versions of the model are estimated for cabinets formed with a populist party as a coalition partner, and for cabinets in which the prime minister belongs to a populist party. The results are also reported separately. The following full model is estimated for each of the real, monetary, and fiscal macro-financial indicators in the Jordà et al. (2017) data:

$$Y_{mct} = \alpha_c + \alpha_t + \alpha_1 Y_{mct-1} + \beta_i \sum_{i=0}^{4} PM_{ct-i} + \beta_j \sum_{j=0}^{4} Cabinet_{ct-j}$$

$$+ \beta_k \sum_{k=0}^{4} CabSeat_{ct-k} + \varepsilon_{mct}, \qquad (4.3)$$

where Y_{mct} is a variable of interest Y_m, varying in country c over time t. By estimating the above equation, we will see if populists in power can affect important macro-variables, as we expect them to. The crucial element in the above model is the PM_{ct} dummy variable, which marks the time in which populists rule country c, with the help of cabinet parties and a certain share of votes in parliament.

A limited version of the model is estimated in which the set of explanatory variables consists of the *Cabinet* dummies as follows:

$$Y_{mct} = \alpha_c + \alpha_t + \alpha_1 Y_{mct-1} + \beta_j \sum_{j=0}^{4} Cabinet_{ct-j} + \varepsilon_{mct}, \qquad (4.4)$$

where the reading of variables is identical to those in Equation (4.3). The standard errors of the estimates are clustered at the country level.

The results from estimating the above models are presented below. They reveal a rich set of political and economic correlates of incumbent populism.

4.4 Results

4.4.1 Political consequences

Table 4.2 and Table 4.3 show the way Freedom in the World ratings react in two scenarios: 1) a government formed with the help of a far-left or a far-right party (Table 4.2), and 2) a government whose prime minister is elected from a far-left or a far-right party (Table 4.3). Even though populists are incumbents in the government in both cases, the two tables clearly demonstrate the difference in the political consequences of populists as junior members of government and populists at the helm of a government. They also illustrate some differences in how far-left and far-right populists approach policy-making.

Table 4.2 exhibits evidence that governments with populist coalition members rarely affect the political process significantly, as Taggart and Rovira Kaltwasser (2016) argue. There is weak evidence that governments with far-left coalition partners weaken political rights almost immediately after assuming power, while governments with far-right coalition partners initially strengthen civil liberties, as indicated in Table 4.2. However, countries with far-right prime ministers experience a much more pronounced worsening of political rights than countries governed by far-left prime ministers over time. This is seen from the PR estimates in Table 4.3. At the same time, the correlation with far-left prime ministers is insignificant throughout the Freedom in the World indices.

Table 4.2 Democracy with Extreme Cabinets (Freedom House Data)

	Far-Left Cabinet Party			Far-Right Cabinet Party		
	PR (1)	*CL (2)*	*NS (3)*	*PR (4)*	*CL (5)*	*NS (6)*
Cabinet$_t$	0.067*	−0.031	−0.007	0.009	−0.137***	−0.019*
	(0.038)	(0.062)	(0.008)	(0.056)	(0.050)	(0.011)
Cabinet$_{t-1}$	−0.054	0.029	−0.001	−0.042	0.016	−0.023
	(0.037)	(0.057)	(0.003)	(0.036)	(0.073)	(0.020)
Cabinet$_{t-2}$	−0.045	0.012	−0.001	−0.024	0.009	0.037
	(0.053)	(0.054)	(0.002)	(0.028)	(0.066)	(0.042)
Cabinet$_{t-3}$	0.059	−0.010	−0.001	−0.077	0.016	0.001
	(0.057)	(0.072)	(0.003)	(0.050)	(0.062)	(0.014)
Cabinet$_{t-4}$	−0.026	−0.101***	−0.007	0.020	−0.073	−0.032*
	(0.037)	(0.033)	(0.005)	(0.046)	(0.044)	(0.017)
Obs.	1160	1160	1160	916	916	916
Adj. R^2	0.206	0.216	0.559	0.126	0.223	0.201

Notes: the table presents results from estimating Equation (4.1) for each of the following variables in the Freedom House (2018) dataset: *Political Rights* (*PR*), *Civil Liberties* (*CL*), and *Numerical Status* (*NS*). *NS* is the numerical equivalent of the original Status index, with F=1, PF=2, and NF=3. Models (1), (2) and (3) estimate Equation (4.1) with a far-left party in government at time t (*Cabinet$_t$=1*) and the *PR*, *CL*, and the *NS* are the dependent variables. Models (4), (5), and (6) estimate Equation (4.1) with a far-right party in government at time t (*Cabinet$_t$=1*) and the *PR*, *CL*, and the *NS* are the dependent variables. Lagged-dependent variables are included in all models, but estimates are not reported. All models include country and time fixed effects. Standard errors are clustered at the country level and are given in parentheses. Symbols: * p <.10, ** p <.05, *** p <.01.

Table 4.3 Democracy with Extreme Prime Ministers (Freedom House Data)

	Far-Left Prime Minister			Far-Right Prime Minister		
	PR (1)	*CL (2)*	*NS (3)*	*PR (4)*	*CL (5)*	*NS (6)*
PM$_t$	0.138	−0.162	−0.073	0.005	0.122	0.022*
	(0.120)	(0.277)	(0.067)	(0.059)	(0.072)	(0.012)
PM$_{t-1}$	−0.115	0.384	0.093	0.085**	−0.007	0.029
	(0.160)	(0.331)	(0.083)	(0.036)	(0.071)	(0.022)
PM$_{t-2}$	0.041	−0.044	−0.012	0.116**	−0.037	−0.026
	(0.111)	(0.053)	(0.012)	(0.045)	(0.062)	(0.037)
PM$_{t-3}$	0.003	−0.102	−0.033	0.182***	−0.028	0.005
	(0.067)	(0.109)	(0.023)	(0.058)	(0.047)	(0.017)
PM$_{t-4}$	0.011	0.187	0.037	0.019	0.108*	0.014
	(0.050)	(0.133)	(0.031)	(0.047)	(0.062)	(0.012)
Obs.	1160	1160	1160	916	916	916
Adj. R^2	0.203	0.228	0.565	0.148	0.224	0.201

Notes: the table presents results from estimating Equation (4.1) for each of the following variables in the Freedom House (2018) dataset: *Political Rights* (*PR*), *Civil Liberties* (*CL*), and *Numerical Status* (*NS*). *NS* is the numerical equivalent of the original Status index, with F=1, PF=2, and NF=3. Models (1), (2), and (3) estimate Equation (4.1) with a far-left prime minister at time t (*PM$_t$=1*) and the *PR*, *CL*, and the *NS* are the dependent variables. Models (4), (5), and (6) estimate Equation (4.1) with a far-right prime minister at time t (*PM$_t$=1*) and the *PR*, *CL* and the *NS* are the dependent variables. Lagged-dependent variables, dummy variables for far-left (far-right) parties in government, and interactions of those dummies with the share of seats occupied by far-left (far-right) parties are included in all models, but estimates are not reported. All models include country and time fixed effects. Standard errors are clustered at the country level and are given in parentheses. Symbols p <.10, ** p <.05, *** p <.01.

Table 4.4 Democracy with Extreme Cabinets (Polity-IV Data)

	Far-Left Cabinet Party			Far-Right Cabinet Party		
	Dem (1)	Aut (2)	P-2 (3)	Dem (4)	Aut (5)	P-2 (6)
Cabinet$_t$	−0.011	0.038	0.141	0.019	0.004	−0.091
	(0.033)	(0.026)	(0.094)	(0.104)	(0.085)	(0.245)
Cabinet$_{t-1}$	0.354	−0.309	0.653	−0.282	0.249	−0.578
	(0.214)	(0.201)	(0.422)	(0.174)	(0.150)	(0.342)
Cabinet$_{t-2}$	−0.348	0.305	−0.522	0.178	−0.167	0.348
	(0.233)	(0.202)	(0.325)	(0.117)	(0.107)	(0.212)
Cabinet$_{t-3}$	0.005	−0.005	−0.142	0.028	−0.033	0.155
	(0.052)	(0.016)	(0.089)	(0.027)	(0.022)	(0.119)
Cabinet$_{t-4}$	−0.046	0.066	−0.152	0.051	−0.023	0.191
	(0.067)	(0.049)	(0.139)	(0.045)	(0.022)	(0.152)
Obs.	1725	1725	1728	1315	1315	1318
Adj. R^2	0.127	0.139	0.201	0.112	0.166	0.188

Notes: the table presents results from estimating Equation (4.1) for each of the following variables in the Marshall et al. (2019) dataset: *Democracy (Dem)*, *Autocracy (Aut)*, and *Polity-2 (P-2)*. Models (1), (2), and (3) estimate Equation (4.1) with a far-left party in government at time t *(Cabinet$_t$=1)* and *Dem*, *Aut*, and *P-2* are the dependent variables. Models (4), (5), and (6) estimate Equation (4.1) with a far-right party in government at time t *(Cabinet$_t$=1)* and *Dem*, *Aut*, and the *P-2* are the dependent variables. Lagged-dependent variables and dummy variables for far-left (far-right) parties in government, are included in all models, but estimates are not reported. All models include country and time fixed effects. Standard errors are clustered at the country level and are given in parentheses. Symbols: * $p < .10$, ** $p < .05$, *** $p < .01$.

In order to evaluate the robustness of the results to the data source, Tables 4.4 and 4.5 apply the same method used in Tables 4.2 and 4.3 to the Polity IV indices. To some extent, the evidence is consistent with the evidence from the Freedom in the World data. Specifically, junior coalition partners do not significantly impact policy-making. This is seen in Table 4.4, in which none of the parameter estimates are significant. However, as before, there is weak evidence that far-right prime ministers strengthen the patterns of autocracy.

The Polity IV data shows a somewhat richer correlation pattern of far-left prime ministers with democracy and autocracy than the Freedom in the World data. Far-left prime ministers are associated with an immediate decrease in the overall Polity index, unlike the far-right prime ministers. However, deeper lags of the PM variable indicate a richer relationship between ruling populists and the state of democracy. Specifically, the second and the fourth lags of the PM dummy show a positive association between far-left populist prime ministers and the overall Polity index. This is consistent with Rovira Kaltwasser (2012, p. 184), who claims that "while populism might well represent a democratic corrective in terms of inclusiveness, it also might become a democratic threat concerning public contestation."

Table 4.5 Democracy with Extreme Prime Ministers (Polity-IV Data)

	Far-Left Prime Minister			Far-Right Prime Minister		
	Dem (1)	*Aut (2)*	*P-2 (3)*	*Dem (4)*	*Aut (5)*	*P-2 (6)*
PM_t	0.172	−0.078	−0.672**	0.090	−0.138	0.356
	(0.101)	(0.071)	(0.304)	(0.169)	(0.152)	(0.398)
PM_{t-1}	−0.247**	0.093	−0.010	0.355*	−0.260*	0.704*
	(0.094)	(0.087)	(0.127)	(0.196)	(0.142)	(0.362)
PM_{t-2}	0.283*	−0.227	0.311*	−0.293	0.227	−0.465
	(0.159)	(0.148)	(0.171)	(0.241)	(0.199)	(0.405)
PM_{t-3}	0.004	0.022	−0.348	0.048	−0.035	−0.136
	(0.093)	(0.082)	(0.326)	(0.071)	(0.071)	(0.165)
PM_{t-4}	−0.069	−0.022	0.368*	−0.146	0.090	−0.486*
	(0.075)	(0.026)	(0.182)	(0.096)	(0.066)	(0.264)
Obs.	1725	1725	1728	1315	1315	1318
Adj. R^2	0.130	0.144	0.220	0.118	0.182	0.218

Notes: the table presents results from estimating Equation (4.1) for each of the following variables in the Marshall et al. (2019) dataset: *Democracy (Dem)*, *Autocracy (Aut)*, and *Polity-2 (P-2)*. Models (1), (2), and (3) estimate Equation (4.1) with a far-left prime minister at time t $(PM_t=1)$ and *Dem*, *Aut*, and *P-2* are the dependent variables. Models (4), (5), and (6) estimate Equation (4.1) with a far-right prime minister at time t $(PM_t=1)$ and *Dem*, *Aut*, and the *P-2* are the dependent variables. Lagged-dependent variables, dummy variables for far-left (far-right) parties in government, and interactions of those dummies with the share of seats occupied by far-left (far-right) parties are included in all models, but estimates are not reported. All models include country and time fixed effects. Standard errors are clustered at the country level and are given in parentheses. Symbols: * $p < .10$, ** $p < .05$, *** $p < .01$.

Populist governance has an ambivalent correlation with democracy, especially across the two main power levels: populists as coalition partners and populists nominating a prime minister. The same is valid for populism's economic consequences. They are discussed next.

4.4.2 Economic consequences

The series of tables in this subsection describe the economic correlates of populism in four repeating sequences: far-left cabinet incumbency, far right cabinet incumbency, far-left prime ministers, and far-right prime ministers. Each of these sequences is applied to the three groups of macro-financial variables published by Jordà et al. (2017): real, monetary, and fiscal.

While the impact of having a populist coalition partner on real macroeconomic dynamics is negligible, and often offsets itself across time, populist prime ministers have a much more pronounced correlation with macroeconomic dynamics. The contrast is easily seen, on the one hand, between Tables 4.6 and 4.7, which demonstrate the irrelevance of incumbent populist parties to the macroeconomy, and Tables 4.8 and 4.9, on the other hand, which tell a largely different story.

Table 4.6 Real Consequences of Far-Left Parties in Government

	RGDPcP (1)	RGDPc (2)	Cons (3)	I/Y (4)	Imp (5)	Exp (6)
Cab.-FL$_t$	−0.007	−0.297	0.574	−0.001	−0.011	−0.096*
	(0.014)	(0.240)	(0.611)	(0.004)	(0.041)	(0.052)
Cab.-FL$_{t-1}$	0.003	0.382	−0.402	−0.012**	0.196	0.015
	(0.021)	(0.522)	(0.477)	(0.005)	(0.113)	(0.050)
Cab.-FL$_{t-2}$	0.019	0.063	−0.979	0.013*	−0.063	0.185**
	(0.019)	(0.433)	(1.040)	(0.007)	(0.091)	(0.085)
Cab.-FL$_{t-3}$	−0.018	−0.197	0.529	0.002	−0.099	−0.120**
	(0.012)	(0.183)	(0.827)	(0.005)	(0.067)	(0.041)
Cab.-FL$_{t-4}$	−0.009	−0.383	−0.231	−0.000	0.054**	0.018
	(0.007)	(0.289)	(0.346)	(0.002)	(0.019)	(0.026)
Obs.	1177	1177	1177	1127	1174	1174
Adj. R^2	0.445	0.527	0.360	0.344	0.613	0.610

Notes: the table presents results from estimating Equation (4.4) for each of the following variables in the Jordà et al. (2017) dataset: log of real GDP per capita in PPP prices (*RGDPcP*), real GDP per capita index (*RGDPc*), real consumption per capita index (*Cons*), investment to GDP ratio (*I/Y*), and the logs of nominal import (*Imp*) and export (*Exp*), as detailed in the source data file. *Cabinet-FL$_t$* means having a far-left party in government in period *t*. Lagged-dependent variables are included in all models, but estimates are not reported. All estimations include country and time fixed effects. Standard errors are clustered at the country level and are given in parentheses. Symbols: * $p < .10$, ** $p < .05$, *** $p < .01$.

Table 4.7 Real Consequences of Far-Right Parties in Government

	RGDPcP (1)	RGDPc (2)	Cons (3)	I/Y (4)	Imp (5)	Exp (6)
Cab-FR$_t$	−0.004	0.027	0.307	−0.004	−0.093	−0.022
	(0.010)	(0.239)	(0.433)	(0.004)	(0.060)	(0.039)
Cab-FR$_{t-1}$	−0.025	−0.375	0.417	0.028**	−0.043	−0.049
	(0.021)	(0.410)	(0.550)	(0.011)	(0.136)	(0.057)
Cab-FR$_{t-2}$	0.001	0.300	−0.780	−0.004	0.105	−0.066
	(0.006)	(0.304)	(0.899)	(0.003)	(0.087)	(0.045)
Cab-FR$_{t-3}$	−0.010	−0.425*	−0.091	−0.014**	−0.017	0.084
	(0.014)	(0.222)	(0.494)	(0.005)	(0.075)	(0.055)
Cab-FR$_{t-4}$	0.021*	0.359	0.313	−0.001	0.023	0.012
	(0.010)	(0.243)	(0.525)	(0.003)	(0.026)	(0.046)
Obs.	870	870	870	827	867	867
Adj. R^2	0.393	0.498	0.360	0.313	0.462	0.563

Notes: the table presents results from estimating Equation (4.4) for each of the following variables in the Jordà et al. (2017) dataset: log of real GDP per capita in PPP prices (*RGDPcP*), real GDP per capita index (*RGDPc*), real consumption per capita index (*Cons*), investment to GDP ratio (*I/Y*), and the logs of nominal import (*Imp*) and export (*Exp*), as detailed in the source data file. *Cab-FR$_t$* means having a far-right party in government in period *t*. Lagged-dependent variables are included in all models, but estimates are not reported. All estimations include country and time fixed effects. Standard errors are clustered at the country level and are given in parentheses. Symbols: * $p < .10$, ** $p < .05$, *** $p < .01$.

Table 4.8 Real Consequences of Far-Left Prime Ministers

	RGDPcP (1)	RGDPc (2)	Cons (3)	I/Y (4)	Imp (5)	Exp (6)
PM-FL$_t$	−0.113***	−2.309***	−3.808***	0.059***	−0.301*	−0.407***
	(0.033)	(0.736)	(0.757)	(0.011)	(0.167)	(0.046)
PM-FL$_{t-1}$	0.060**	2.104***	2.992***	−0.051***	0.145	0.285**
	(0.025)	(0.565)	(0.820)	(0.005)	(0.182)	(0.103)
PM-FL$_{t-2}$	0.030	−0.652	0.641	0.003	−0.365**	−0.583***
	(0.020)	(0.581)	(1.064)	(0.010)	(0.139)	(0.085)
PM-FL$_{t-3}$	0.055***	2.433***	0.405	0.048***	0.316***	0.409***
	(0.013)	(0.235)	(0.800)	(0.005)	(0.063)	(0.073)
PM-FL$_{t-4}$	−0.053***	−2.133***	−0.970***	−0.044***	−0.460***	−0.567***
	(0.008)	(0.391)	(0.265)	(0.004)	(0.034)	(0.038)
Obs.	1177	1177	1177	1127	1174	1174
Adj. R^2	0.460	0.527	0.366	0.355	0.635	0.641

Notes: the table presents results from estimating Equation (4.3) for each of the following variables in the Jordà et al. (2017) dataset: log of real GDP per capita in PPP prices (*RGDPcP*), real GDP per capita index (*RGDPc*), real consumption per capita index (*Cons*), investment to GDP ratio (*I/Y*), and the logs of nominal import (*Imp*) and export (*Exp*), as detailed in the source data file. *PM-FL$_t$* means having a far-left prime minister in period *t*. Lagged-dependent variables, dummy variables for far-left parties in government, and interactions of those dummies with the share of seats occupied by far-left parties are included in all models, but estimates are not reported. All estimations include country and time fixed effects. Standard errors are clustered at the country level and are given in parentheses. Symbols: * $p <.10$, ** $p <.05$, *** $p <.01$.

Table 4.9 Real Consequences of Far-Right Prime Ministers

	RGDPcP (1)	RGDPc (2)	Cons (3)	I/Y (4)	Imp (5)	Exp (6)
PM-FR$_t$	0.046**	1.157***	1.308***	0.039	0.184**	0.064
	(0.018)	(0.343)	(0.410)	(0.024)	(0.066)	(0.059)
PM-FR$_{t-1}$	0.014	−0.258	−0.812	0.000	0.008	−0.010
	(0.023)	(0.305)	(0.670)	(0.013)	(0.133)	(0.055)
PM-FR$_{t-2}$	0.003	−0.284	2.623	−0.079*	0.317**	0.185
	(0.020)	(0.538)	(1.833)	(0.039)	(0.141)	(0.113)
PM-FR$_{t-3}$	−0.085**	−1.060*	−2.188*	0.027**	−0.411***	−0.337***
	(0.039)	(0.494)	(1.085)	(0.010)	(0.124)	(0.107)
PM-FR$_{t-4}$	0.040*	0.527	0.091	0.009	0.018	0.229***
	(0.020)	(0.305)	(0.468)	(0.014)	(0.041)	(0.066)
Obs.	870	870	870	827	867	867
Adj. R^2	0.425	0.500	0.376	0.394	0.508	0.577

Notes: the table presents results from estimating Equation (4.3) for each of the following variables in the Jordà et al. (2017) dataset: log of real GDP per capita in PPP prices(*RGDPcP*), real GDP per capita index (*RGDPc*), real consumption per capita index (*Cons*), investment to GDP ratio (*I/Y*), and the logs of nominal import (*Imp*) and export (*Exp*), as detailed in the source data file. *PM-FR$_t$* means having a far-right prime minister in period *t*. Lagged-dependent variables, dummy variables for far-right parties in government, and interactions of those dummies with the share of seats occupied by far-left parties are included in all models, but estimates are not reported. All estimations include country and time fixed effects. Standard errors are clustered at the country level and are given in parentheses. Symbols: * $p <.10$, ** $p <.05$, *** $p <.01$.

Far-left and far-right prime ministers are different in terms of how their policies affect the macroeconomy. Governments led by a far-left politician are associated with lower GDP per capita, less consumption and trade, and a slightly higher share of investment in GDP, relative to the other economies. Governments led by a far-right politician correlate positively with average income levels, consumption, and trade. Whatever the differences between the real effects of extreme prime ministers, the longer they stay in power, the higher the chances are that their policies will activate a decline in the macroeconomy. This is seen from the PM-FL$_{t-4}$ estimates in Table 4.8 and PM-FR$_{t-3}$ estimates in Table 4.9.

The conclusion above is similar to those of Cachanosky and Padilla (2019). They find a significant decrease in income per capita and in human development indices in five Latin American countries run by populist governments – Argentina, Bolivia, Ecuador, Nicaragua, and Venezuela. Although their sample is small, the empirical approach they have taken is a promising one for future research, not only for GDP per capita and human development, but also for many other macro-correlates of populist rule.

The monetary correlates of extreme party incumbency also differ along the degree of influence populists hold in a government. This is seen in two sets of tables. Tables 4.10 and 4.11 show the correlations between monetary aggregates, interest rates, and an extreme left or an extreme right coalition party in government. Tables 4.12 and 4.13 demonstrate the same correlations with an extreme prime minister.

Table 4.10 Monetary Consequences of Far-Left Parties in Government

	N-Money (1)	B-Money (2)	STNIR (3)	LTNIR (4)
Cab-FL$_t$	−0.032***	−0.016	0.135	0.048
	(0.008)	(0.010)	(0.276)	(0.116)
Cab-FL$_{t-1}$	−0.023	−0.026**	−0.191*	0.058
	(0.014)	(0.010)	(0.097)	(0.047)
Cab-FL$_{t-2}$	0.057**	0.037**	−0.135	−0.089
	(0.024)	(0.015)	(0.202)	(0.092)
Cab-FL$_{t-3}$	−0.007	−0.003	0.020	−0.116
	(0.023)	(0.006)	(0.152)	(0.104)
Cab-FL$_{t-4}$	−0.030**	−0.018*	−0.107	0.119
	(0.012)	(0.009)	(0.098)	(0.126)
Obs.	1154	1116	1159	1167
Adj. R^2	0.254	0.409	0.404	0.392

Notes: the table presents results from estimating Equation (4.4) for each of the following variables in the Jordà et al. (2017) dataset: narrow money (*N-Money*), broad money (*B-Money*), short-term nominal interest rates (*STNIR*), and long-term nominal interest rates (*LTNIR*), as detailed in the source data file. *Cab-FL$_t$* means having a far-left party in government in period *t*. Lagged-dependent variables are included in all models, but estimates are not reported. All estimations include country and time fixed effects. Standard errors are clustered at the country level and are given in parentheses. Symbols: * $p <.10$, ** $p <.05$, *** $p <.01$.

Table 4.11 Monetary Consequences of Far-Right Parties in Government

	N-Money (1)	B-Money (2)	STNIR (3)	LTNIR (4)
Cab-FR$_t$	0.008	0.008	−0.002	−0.175
	(0.016)	(0.007)	(0.285)	(0.133)
Cab-FR$_{t-1}$	0.015	−0.001	−0.538*	−0.210
	(0.022)	(0.011)	(0.281)	(0.163)
Cab-FR$_{t-2}$	−0.044	−0.016	0.727**	0.397***
	(0.029)	(0.013)	(0.241)	(0.102)
Cab-FR$_{t-3}$	−0.048*	−0.009	−0.115	0.137
	(0.027)	(0.023)	(0.317)	(0.180)
Cab-FR$_{t-4}$	0.033**	0.025**	0.017	−0.047
	(0.015)	(0.011)	(0.211)	(0.125)
Obs.	847	819	858	870
Adj. R^2	0.215	0.312	0.497	0.538

Notes: the table presents results from estimating Equation (4.4) for each of the following variables in the Jordà et al. (2017) dataset: narrow money (*N-Money*), broad money (*B-Money*), short-term nominal interest rates (*STNIR*), and long-term nominal interest rates (*LTNIR*), as detailed in the source data file. *Cab-FR$_t$* means having a far-right party in government in period *t*. Lagged-dependent variables are included in all models, but estimates are not reported. All estimations include country and time fixed effects. Standard errors are clustered at the country level and are given in parentheses. Symbols: * $p <.10$, ** $p <.05$, *** $p <.01$.

Table 4.12 Monetary Consequences of Far-Left Prime Ministers

	N-Money (1)	B-Money (2)	STNIR (3)	LTNIR (4)
PM-FL$_t$	−0.032	−0.044**	−0.908***	0.070
	(0.029)	(0.016)	(0.149)	(0.134)
PM-FL$_{t-1}$	−0.032	−0.088***	1.449***	0.017
	(0.026)	(0.026)	(0.181)	(0.159)
PM-FL$_{t-2}$	−0.069*	−0.059***	−1.255***	0.217
	(0.034)	(0.017)	(0.326)	(0.168)
PM-FL$_{t-3}$	−0.064***	−0.155***	0.968***	−0.136
	(0.019)	(0.023)	(0.211)	(0.111)
PM-FL$_{t-4}$	0.000	0.000	−0.621***	0.064
	(.)	(.)	(0.128)	(0.124)
Obs.	1154	1116	1159	1167
Adj. R^2	0.260	0.429	0.399	0.392

Notes: the table presents results from estimating Equation (4.3) for each of the following variables in the Jordà et al. (2017) dataset: narrow money (*N-Money*), broad money (*B-Money*), short-term nominal interest rates (*STNIR*), and long-term nominal interest rates (*LTNIR*), as detailed in the source data file. *PM-FL$_t$* means having a far-left prime minister in period *t*. Lagged-dependent variables, dummy variables for far-left parties in government, and interactions of those dummies with the share of seats occupied by far-left parties are included in all models, but estimates are not reported. All estimations include country and time fixed effects. Standard errors are clustered at the country level and are given in parentheses. Symbols: * $p <.10$, ** $p <.05$, *** $p <.01$.

Table 4.13 Monetary Consequences of Far-Right Prime Ministers

	N-Money (1)	B-Money (2)	STNIR (3)	LTNIR (4)
PM-FR$_t$	−0.025	−0.030	0.159	−0.348***
	(0.030)	(0.019)	(0.194)	(0.113)
PM-FR$_{t-1}$	0.058	0.036	−0.450	0.397***
	(0.065)	(0.042)	(0.393)	(0.128)
PM-FR$_{t-2}$	0.110*	0.068*	−0.315	−0.152
	(0.054)	(0.033)	(0.743)	(0.264)
PM-FR$_{t-3}$	−0.083	−0.036	0.414	0.121
	(0.055)	(0.026)	(1.014)	(0.516)
PM-FR$_{t-4}$	−0.024	−0.038**	0.155	−0.112
	(0.034)	(0.013)	(0.432)	(0.256)
Obs.	847	819	858	870
Adj. R^2	0.226	0.328	0.492	0.535

Notes: the table presents results from estimating Equation (4.3) for each of the following variables in the Jordà et al. (2017) dataset: narrow money (*N-Money*), broad money (*B-Money*), short-term nominal interest rates (*STNIR*), and long-term nominal interest rates (*LTNIR*), as detailed in the source data file. *PM-FR$_t$* means having a far-right prime minister in period *t*. Lagged-dependent variables, dummy variables for far-right parties in government, and interactions of those dummies with the share of seats occupied by far-right parties are included in all models, but estimates are not reported. All estimations include country and time fixed effects. Standard errors are clustered at the country level and are given in parentheses. Symbols: * p <.10, ** p <.05, *** p <.01.

Based on the long history of populism in Latin America, I expected to see a correlation of far-left incumbent populists with rapid expansion of the monetary base and lower interest rates. In fact, what can be observed in the *ParlGov* sample of 33 developed economies is the opposite. More often than not, governments formed with the support of far-left parties end up shrinking the monetary base, and do not exert any significant impact on either short- or long-term interest rates. The evidence for far-right parties in governments is inconclusive in the short-run, with little significance of the correlation coefficients before the second lags of the *CAB-FR* dummies. The deeper lags emerge as significant at 5% level: both short-term and long-term interest rates increase about two years after a government is formed with the help of far-right populists.

Unlike the cabinet dummies, many prime minister dummies for far-left governments appear to be significant, as seen from Tables 4.12 and 4.13. They demonstrate that far-left governments in Europe and OECD countries are associated with monetary contractions, contrary to their Latin American counterparts. Note, however, that the sample size of 6 far-left PMs in Europe and the OECD is not strongly informative on underlying patterns of far-left monetary policy-making. In addition, we know that in Europe and the OECD, monetary policy authorities are significantly more

Table 4.14 Fiscal Consequences of Far-Left Parties in Government

	D/GDP (1)	GRev (2)	GExp (3)	XRate (4)	Crisis (5)
Cab-FL$_t$	−0.023	−0.018	−0.020	−18.851	0.009
	(0.019)	(0.031)	(0.041)	(17.771)	(0.007)
Cab-FL$_{t-1}$	−0.005	0.040*	0.123*	30.719	−0.011
	(0.010)	(0.021)	(0.058)	(29.378)	(0.009)
Cab-FL$_{t-2}$	−0.000	−0.001	−0.017	3.729	0.022
	(0.026)	(0.035)	(0.055)	(4.862)	(0.025)
Cab-FL$_{t-3}$	0.006	−0.013	−0.027	−14.749	−0.025
	(0.012)	(0.036)	(0.056)	(14.417)	(0.017)
Cab-FL$_{t-4}$	0.010	−0.008	−0.012	0.590	0.005
	(0.012)	(0.016)	(0.024)	(5.120)	(0.010)
Obs.	1121	1152	1173	1177	1177
Adj. R^2	0.278	0.414	0.360	0.031	0.677

Notes: the table presents results from estimating Equation (4.4) for each of the following variables in the Jordà et al. (2017) dataset: public debt to GDP ratio (*D/GDP*), log of nominal government revenues (*GRev*), log of nominal government expenditures (*GExp*), local currency exchange rate with the USD: Local/USD (*XRate*), and a dummy variable indicating a systemic financial crisis (*Crisis*), as detailed in the source data file. *Cab-FL$_t$* means having a far-left party in government in period *t*. Lagged-dependent variables are included in all models, but estimates are not reported. All estimations include country and time fixed effects. Standard errors are clustered at the country level and are given in parentheses. Symbols: * $p < .10$, ** $p < .05$, *** $p < .01$.

independent than those in Latin America (Cukierman et al., 1992; Garriga, 2016). Therefore, far-left governments may simply coincide with restrictive monetary cycles rather than being drivers of them.

Far-left and far-right coalition parties in governments in developed countries are also not significantly correlated with changes in fiscal policies. This is in contrast with earlier evidence for Western Europe by Bernhard and Kriesi (2019). There is some weak evidence that the presence of far-left parties in government increases both government revenues and expenditures (Table 4.14), and that far-right parties correlate with initial reductions of government expenditures and debt levels (Table 4.15).

Much stronger evidence emerges of a fiscal impact of far-left prime ministers, as seen in Table 4.16. However, the changing dynamics of the correlation over time does not provide compelling evidence of an overall direction of populist fiscal policies in Europe and the OECD countries. Similarly inconclusive information is evident in Table 4.17, which shows the correlations of far-right prime ministers with fiscal policy parameters.

The ambiguous fiscal and monetary policy evidence is supportive of earlier conclusions by Havlík (2019) and Toplišek (2020), who analyze populist governments in post-crisis Czech Republic, Hungary, and Poland. They do not find enough support for a classic *populist paradigm* shift in

Table 4.15 Fiscal Consequences of Far-Right Parties in Government

	D/GDP (1)	GRev (2)	GExp (3)	XRate (4)	Crisis (5)
Cab-FR$_t$	−0.042*	−0.013	0.012	4.646	−0.016
	(0.020)	(0.029)	(0.038)	(5.036)	(0.019)
Cab-FR$_{t-1}$	0.082*	−0.056	−0.082**	−0.928	0.022
	(0.038)	(0.032)	(0.034)	(2.348)	(0.021)
Cab-FR$_{t-2}$	−0.127	0.029	0.025	−0.263	−0.034
	(0.076)	(0.016)	(0.021)	(1.732)	(0.039)
Cab-FR$_{t-3}$	0.058***	0.008	−0.020	−1.742	0.037
	(0.017)	(0.027)	(0.026)	(4.321)	(0.046)
Cab-FR$_{t-4}$	0.019	0.021	0.064	1.543	−0.007
	(0.026)	(0.013)	(0.042)	(2.690)	(0.019)
Obs.	822	858	868	870	870
Adj. R^2	0.363	0.375	0.415	−0.006	0.666

Notes: the table presents results from estimating Equation (4.4) for each of the following variables in the Jordà et al. (2017) dataset: public debt to GDP ratio (*D/GDP*), log of nominal government revenues (*GRev*), log of nominal government expenditures (*GExp*), local currency exchange rate with the USD: Local/USD (*XRate*), and a dummy variable indicating a systemic financial crisis (*Crisis*), as detailed in the source data file. *Cab-FR$_t$* means having a far-left party in government in period *t*. Lagged-dependent variables are included in all models, but estimates are not reported. All estimations include country and time fixed effects. Standard errors are clustered at the country level and are given in parentheses. Symbols: * *p* <.10, ** *p* <.05, *** *p* <.01.

Table 4.16 Fiscal Consequences of Far-Left Prime Ministers

	D/GDP (1)	GRev (2)	GExp (3)	XRate (4)	Crisis (5)
PM-FL$_t$	−0.014	0.416***	1.147***	7.180	−0.029
	(0.015)	(0.042)	(0.078)	(16.225)	(0.030)
PM-FL$_{t-1}$	−0.012	−0.229***	−1.014***	−11.453	0.046
	(0.021)	(0.037)	(0.052)	(15.025)	(0.029)
PM-FL$_{t-2}$	−0.066**	0.226***	0.975***	−14.648*	−0.013
	(0.026)	(0.038)	(0.066)	(6.975)	(0.033)
PM-FL$_{t-3}$	0.028*	−0.229***	−0.977***	22.040	0.027
	(0.014)	(0.043)	(0.024)	(16.227)	(0.023)
PM-FL$_{t-4}$	0.000	0.174***	0.933***	−2.320	0.013
	(.)	(0.026)	(0.053)	(2.917)	(0.010)
Obs.	1121	1152	1173	1177	1177
Adj. R^2	0.276	0.442	0.400	0.027	0.674

Notes: the table presents results from estimating Equation (4.3) for each of the following variables in the Jordà et al. (2017) dataset: public debt to GDP ratio (D/GDP), log of nominal government revenues (*GRev*), log of nominal government expenditures (*GExp*), local currency exchange rate with the USD: Local/USD (*XRate*), and a dummy variable indicating a systemic financial crisis (*Crisis*), as detailed in the source data file. *PM-FL$_t$* means having a far-left prime minister in period *t*. Lagged-dependent variables, dummy variables for far-left parties in government, and interactions of those dummies with the share of seats occupied by far-left parties are included in all models, but estimates are not reported. All estimations include country and time fixed effects. Standard errors are clustered at the country level and are given in parentheses. Symbols: * *p* <.10, ** *p* <.05, *** *p* <.01.

Table 4.17 Fiscal Consequences of Far-Right Prime Ministers

	D/GDP (1)	GRev (2)	GExp (3)	XRate (4)	Crisis (5)
PM-FR$_t$	−0.038	0.072	0.080	4.616	−0.035
	(0.039)	(0.055)	(0.084)	(7.021)	(0.040)
PM-FR$_{t-1}$	0.102	0.022	0.005	−2.411	0.008
	(0.064)	(0.052)	(0.069)	(3.554)	(0.097)
PM-FR$_{t-2}$	−0.242**	−0.002	0.017	−4.631	−0.140
	(0.103)	(0.043)	(0.047)	(6.434)	(0.166)
PM-FR$_{t-3}$	0.223***	−0.041	−0.009	3.116	0.052
	(0.052)	(0.059)	(0.043)	(4.049)	(0.167)
PM-FR$_{t-4}$	0.010	−0.015	−0.077***	−4.004	0.041
	(0.052)	(0.023)	(0.017)	(4.557)	(0.062)
Obs.	822	858	868	870	870
Adj. R^2	0.458	0.386	0.432	−0.019	0.666

Notes: the table presents results from estimating Equation (4.3) for each of the following variables in the Jordà et al. (2017) dataset: public debt to GDP ratio (*D/GDP*), log of nominal government revenues (*GRev*), log of nominal government expenditures (*GExp*), local currency exchange rate with the USD: Local/USD (*XRate*), and a dummy variable indicating a systemic financial crisis (*Crisis*), as detailed in the source data file. *PM-FR$_t$* means having a far-right prime minister in period *t*. Lagged-dependent variables, dummy variables for far-right parties in government, and interactions of those dummies with the share of seats occupied by far-right parties are included in all models, but estimates are not reported. All estimations include country and time fixed effects. Standard errors are clustered at the country level and are given in parentheses. Symbols: * $p < .10$, ** $p < .05$, *** $p < .01$.

economic policies often seen in Latin America, which recent evidence relates to a short-lived growth followed by a rapid decline (Ball et al., 2019).

The results above naturally lead to some broad conclusions about how populism operates, and what voters and mainstream parties can do to stem its inevitable rise. They are presented next.

Note

1 The full methodological description is available at https://freedomhouse.org/

Bibliography

Acemoglu, D., Egorov, G., & Sonin, K. (2013). A political theory of populism. *The Quarterly Journal of Economics*, *128*(2), 771–805.

Alesina, A., & Passalacqua, A. (2015). The political economy of government debt. Working Paper 21821, National Bureau of Economic Research.

Bakker, R., de Vries, C., Edwards, E., Hooghe, L., Jolly, S., Marks, G., & Vachudova, M. A. (2015). Measuring party positions in Europe: The chapel hill expert survey trend file, 1999–2010. *Party Politics*, *21*(1), 143–152.

Ball, C., Freytag, A., & Kautz, M. (2019). Populism-what next? A first look at populist walking-stick economies. CESifo Working Paper Series 7914, CESifo Group Munich.

Batory, A. (2016). Populists in government? Hungary's "system of national cooperation". *Democratization, 23*(2), 283–303.

Benoit, K., & Laver, M. (2006). *Party policy in modern democracies*. Routledge Research in Comparative Politics. Routledge.

Bernhard, L., & Kriesi, H. (2019). Populism in election times: A comparative analysis of 11 countries in Western Europe. *Western European Politics, 42*(6), 1188–1208.

Bogaards, M. (2009). How to classify hybrid regimes? Defective democracy and electoral authoritarianism. *Democratization, 16*(2), 399–423.

Brewer-Carías, A. (2010). *Dismantling democracy in Venezuela: The Chávez authoritarian experiment*. Cambridge University Press.

Buchanan, J., & Wagner, R. (1977). *Democracy in deficit: The political legacy of Lord Keynes*. Academic Press.

Cachanosky, N., & Padilla, A. (2019). A panel data analysis of Latin American populism. Technical Report, Metropolitan State University of Denver, Economics Department. Mimeo.

Castles, F. G., & Mair, P. (1984). Left-right political scales: Some 'expert' judgments. *European Journal of political Research, 12*(1), 73–88.

Cianetti, L., Dawson, J., & Hanley, S. (2018). Rethinking "democratic backsliding" in Central and Eastern Europe – Looking beyond Hungary and Poland. *East European Politics, 34*(3), 243–256.

Colburn, F. D. (2011). Dismantling democracy in Venezuela: The Chávez authoritarian experiment. *Perspectives on Politics, 9*(3), 733–734.

Cukierman, A., Webb, S. B., & Neyapti, B. (1992). Measuring the independence of central banks and its effect on policy outcomes. *The World Bank Economic Review, 6*(3), 353–398.

Dalio, R., Kryger, S., Rogers, J., & Davis, G. (2017). Populism: The phenomenon. Technical Report 3/22/2017, Bridgewater Associates, LP.

de la Torre, C., & Lemos, A. O. (2016). Populist polarization and the slow death of democracy in Ecuador. *Democratization, 23*(2), 221–241.

Denisova, A. (2017). Democracy, protest and public sphere in Russia after the 2011–2012 anti-government protests: Digital media at stake. *Media, Culture and Society, 39*(7), 976–994.

Döring, H., & Manow, P. (2019). Parliaments and governments database (parlgov): Information on parties, elections and cabinets in modern democracies. Accessed September 29, 2019 from http://www.parlgov.org/

Dornbusch, R., & Edwards, S. (1990). Macroeconomic populism. *Journal of Development Economics, 32*(2), 247–277.

Dornbusch, R., & Edwards, S. (1991a). Introduction to *The Macroeconomics of Populism in Latin America*. In R. Dornbusch & S. Edwards (Eds.), *The macroeconomics of populism in Latin America* (pp. 1–4). University of Chicago Press.

Dornbusch, R., & Edwards, S. (1991b). *The macroeconomics of populism in Latin America*. University of Chicago Press.

Dovis, A., Golosov, M., & Shourideh, A. (2016). Political economy of sovereign debt: A theory of cycles of populism and austerity. Working Paper 21948, National Bureau of Economic Research.

Downs, A. (1957). An economic theory of political action in a democracy. *Journal of Political Economy*, *65*(2), 135–150.

Evans, A. B. (2011). The failure of democratization in Russia: A comparative perspective. *Journal of Eurasian Studies*, *2*(1), 40–51.

Freedom House. (2018). Freedom in the world, 1973–2018. Retrieved November 12, 2019 from https://freedomhouse.org/

Garriga, A. C. (2016). Central Bank independence in the world: A new data set. *International Interactions*, *42*(5), 849–868.

Havlík, V. (2019). Technocratic populism and political illiberalism in Central Europe. *Problems of Post-Communism*, *66*(6), 369–384.

Huber, J., & Inglehart, R. (1995). Expert interpretations of party space and party locations in 42 societies. *Party Politics*, *1*(1), 73–111.

Jordà, O., Schularick, M., & Taylor, A. M. (2017). Macrofinancial history and the new business cycle facts. In M. Eichenbaum and J. A. Parker (Eds.), *NBER Macroeconomics Annual 2016, Volume 31*, pp. 213–263. University of Chicago Press.

Kendall-Taylor, A., Lindstaedt, N., & Frantz, E. (2019). *Democracies and authoritarian regimes*. Oxford University Press.

Marshall, M. G., Gurr, T. R., & Jaggers, K. (2019). Polity IV project. Political regime characteristics and transitions, 1800–2018. Retrieved December 9, 2019 from http://www.systemicpeace.org/inscrdata.html

Matthes, C.-Y. (2016). The state of democracy in Poland after 2007. *Problems of Post-Communism*, *63*(5–6), 288–299.

Mian, A., Sufi, A., & Trebbi, F. (2014). Resolving debt overhang: Political constraints in the aftermath of financial crises. *American Economic Journal: Macroeconomics*, *6*(2), 1–28.

Ochsner, C., & Rösel, F. (2016). Migrating extremists. CESifo Working Paper Series 5799, CESifo Group Munich.

Pehe, J. (2018). Explaining Eastern Europe: Czech democracy under pressure. *Journal of Democracy*, *29*(3), 65–77.

Rode, M., & Revuelta, J. (2015). The wild bunch! An empirical note on populism and economic institutions. *Economics of Governance 16*(1), 73–96.

Rovira Kaltwasser, C. (2012). The ambivalence of populism: Threat and corrective for democracy. *Democratization*, *19*(2), 184–208.

Saboin-Garcia, J. L. (2018). The modern hyperinflation cycle: Some new empirical regularities. IMF Working Papers 18/266, International Monetary Fund.

Sakwa, R. (2011). The future of Russian democracy. *Government and Opposition*, *46*(4), 517–537.

Stankov, P. (2017). Crises, welfare, and populism. In *Economic freedom and welfare before and after the crisis* (pp. 135–164). Cham: Springer International Publishing.

Stankov, P. (2018). The political economy of populism: An empirical investigation. *Comparative Economic Studies, 60*(2), 230–253.

Taggart, P., & Rovira Kaltwasser, C. (2016). Dealing with populists in government: Some comparative conclusions. *Democratization, 23*(2), 345–365.

Toplišek, A. (2020). The political economy of populist rule in post-crisis Europe: Hungary and Poland. *New Political Economy, 25*(3), 388–403.

5 What can we do about populism?

Populism emerges and gains traction when political entrepreneurs with strong leadership qualities explore already existing identity conflicts. The search for political gains is more likely to succeed in times of economic transformations because recessions, austerity, and inequality produce a variety of distributional consequences. As the distributional consequences of both economic distress and economic growth typically favor the elite over the poor and the lower middle class, economic shocks typically sharpen the underlying identity conflicts, and identity rents become a more salient characteristic of voter choice at both the extensive and the intensive margins.

Despite those conflicts, liberal-democratic systems uniquely harbor the power of self-correction (Galston, 2018, p. 5). Is today's populism part of the liberal-democratic self-correcting mechanism, or it is a prelude to its demise? This book has shown that populist governance has an ambivalent correlation with democracy. Earlier case studies have found that populists have tended to undermine democracy, especially in Latin America and in countries with shorter democratic traditions. However, the empirical evidence in this book suggests a more nuanced relationship, particularly in Europe and in the OECD countries.

In addition, incumbent populism takes two forms with distinctly different impacts on policy-making. When populists serve as junior coalition partners, they are usually unable to significantly affect either the democratic process or economic policy-making, in line with conjectures by Taggart and Rovira Kaltwasser (2016). However, a populist prime minister exerts a much more pronounced control over both.

Far-left and far-right prime ministers are different in terms of how their policies affect the macroeconomy. Governments led by a far-left politician usually precede a macroeconomic decline, while governments in Europe and the OECD led by a far-right politician typically correlate positively with consumption, average income, and trade. Whatever the differences between the real effects of extreme left or extreme right prime ministers, the longer they stay in power, the higher the risks are that their policies will result in economic decline.

Further, there is evidence of significant differences in the ways fiscal and monetary policies are conducted by incumbent populists in Latin America, on the one hand, and in Europe and the OECD, on the other hand. In Latin America, policies fit the populist paradigm (Dornbusch and Edwards, 1990). In the developed world, they tend to be far less destructive, and in some cases are conducive to economic growth.

Economic growth, however, does not guarantee the disappearance of populism. Growth periods create more demand for a migrant labor force. As most migration is economic rather than political, periods of growth coincide with larger inflows of immigrants. Voters who perceive immigrants as different from themselves experience identity costs which may well outweigh the value added of migrants to the local economy. Further, immigration has distributional consequences – typically, high-skilled and richer individuals and firms benefit more from immigration than low-skilled workers.

Therefore, even though the local economy benefits from immigration, which makes the average worker better off, a significant portion of the electorate does not experience those benefits. As a result, because of the dominance of identity costs over material benefits from immigration, periods of growth also increase the appetite for populism among large segments of the electorate. Exogenous migration shocks in other parts of the world such as wars, drought, and famine can increase the number of asylum-seekers in countries with well-developed social welfare systems, which further escalates the identity losses for both the rich and the poor.

To limit political backlashes against immigration, and a resulting rise of populism to the mainstream, two types of policies, which directly address the identity costs of immigration imposed on the low-skilled workers, can be applied. First, banning migration is never optimal. However, limiting immigrants' access to the social welfare system will render free immigration politically optimal. If this type of limitation is not feasible, then constraining low-skilled and encouraging high-skilled migration can prevent or reduce dissonance costs. Explicit policies addressing identity costs have to date not been included in mainstream political platforms, but we may soon see them being applied.

From a normative perspective, a narrow focus on identity costs would be an incomplete and ineffective policy response to the rising populism. Because trade and entry liberalization alter supply chains on a global scale, dying industries in Western democracies produce structural unemployment, which has lasting labor market implications, particularly for low-skilled and less educated workers. The unprecedented speed of contemporary technological progress is geared towards rewarding the high-skilled, and aggravates income inequality. Then, labor market assistance programs for globalization's losers can tangibly increase their rents from globalization by dampening the impact of globalization on identity costs, and raising their material benefits from it.

Designing such compensation programs, however, requires learning from the past failures of populism. Ignoring sound macroeconomic policies may work in the short-term to stem the rise of social discontent, but ultimately ends up in economic collapse, hurting the very people who need government assistance most. Recurring cycles of left-wing populist euphoria and fatigue in Latin America have demonstrated that pure redistribution of "the pie" without expanding its size do not deliver on the populist promise of restoring social justice. However, policy fixations with growth and technological progress will not stem the rise of populists, because they ignore the impact of inequitable growth and radical innovation on identity rents. Therefore, we need a new vision for 21st century redistribution platforms.

An economic redistribution platform for the 21st century stands on three broad pillars of a new social consensus: wealth, technology, and the environment. Faced with a credible threat of systemic political change based on radical income redistribution, the elite may find it rational to choose the lesser of two evils: a wealth-sharing mechanism financing social welfare programs for the poor on a scale comparable to the post-war Western European welfare state. Note that the first modern welfare reform was the German universal Health Insurance Law, which Otto von Bismarck introduced in 1883 to stymie rising political conflict with the radical socialists of the time. Reforms in our day will be very different, but their political motivations and effects may nonetheless be equivalent.

For example, based on recent and earlier academic work (Piketty, 2015; Saez and Zucman, 2019), proposals of a wealth tax reform are gaining prominence in the developed world. Despite valid criticisms of the proposals (Auerbach and Hassett, 2015; Mankiw, 2015), a wealth tax is marching into the 2020 US Democratic Party candidate platforms (Wessel, 2019). In addition, a wealth tax can help to bridge the identity gap between the rich and the poor – the rich would share the spoils of growth and globalization, thereby contributing to the less well-off segments of their nation, while the poor would perceive that they are treated more fairly.

A wealth tax can work under two conditions. First, its proceeds need to directly contribute to the livelihoods of poor and lower middle-class citizens through housing and education programs. This can bolster political support for further wealth-creation reforms, as the poor will experience the benefits of trickle-down economics again. Second, to limit evasion by the rich, a wealth tax should ideally be coordinated on an international scale similar to the United Nations Framework Convention on Climate Change. Environmental protocols have proven difficult, but not impossible to coordinate, especially when heads of governments realize that pursuing their dominant, self-centered strategies leads to socially inferior outcomes.

At the same time, the radical technological progress of our time has created an entirely new class of "workers": robots. As the costs of automation fall, displacement of traditional workers will continue at an accelerated pace. The resulting structural unemployment on the transition path to an automated world will continue to pose economic and social challenges. If left unaddressed, these will quickly morph into political problems. This is both because the economy is moving to an automated equilibrium faster than policies suited for such equilibrium, and because in a political world dominated by social networks, political preferences adjust far more quickly than policies. Thus, the demand side of a political market may rapidly shift to a pure redistribution stance not seen since the second half of the 19th century.

No-one disputes the value of automation to economic growth. Yet, automation potentially carries distributional consequences similar to those generated by the first industrial revolution in the 19th century. Back then, revolutionary far-left academic efforts that emerged in the mid-19th century had slowly made their way into the political mainstream by the early 20th century, with devastating economic and political consequences for hundreds of millions. Today, social networks have radically reduced the costs of organizing large masses of people. As a result, the 21st-century path to the mainstream of similarly destructive ideas could be far shorter. Therefore, there is a need for policies to address the inequality issues created by automation.

There are two ways to address the distributional consequences of automation now. First, the value added by automation could be spent to design and support a 21st-century education system, which supplies the labor market with more creators and fewer imitators. A reform of this sort would require continuing education opportunities all along the working life-cycle, and would be more focused on cutting-edge industry and technology than on classroom theory. Education reforms geared towards innovation could address the increasingly narrowing opportunities for social mobility in many developed nations. Second, automation will leave older generations of workers less equipped to deal with the rapidly adjusting industry demand for new skills. Then, a gradual phase-in of the universal basic income (UBI) down the age ladder would ensure partial compensation for the older workers.

Developing countries may not see the benefits of the automation revolution until much later in the future, in line with the Lucas "Paradox" (Lucas, 1990). Because of their poorer institutional environment (Alfaro et al., 2008), poorer nations may fall behind on a scale comparable to the income divergence brought about by the first industrial revolution. This would trigger further migration to developed countries and strain their already volatile political systems.

To alleviate the strain, direct aid programs have been designed in the past. However, they have had controversial effects for most developing countries (Djankov et al., 2008), and could therefore be re-evaluated and phased out. Then, assistance programs to bring human capital generated in Western education systems to the developing world may prove beneficial. This could work if those assistance programs are complemented by institutional convergence measures between the developed and the developing world. European Union proposals to tie its cohesion policies to the rule of law environment in recipient countries is just one example of the many incentive-compatible ways to stimulate institutional convergence across countries.

However, institutional convergence reforms need to be tailored to the local context. A shock adoption of the Western-style institutional framework may face severe local political economy constraints, and even if it goes through, it may still produce a variety of reform outcomes across countries (Stankov and Vasilev, 2019). Importantly, if those reforms do not compensate the losers, they can result in further increases in the demand for and supply of populists, just as in earlier historical episodes.

Besley and Persson (2019, p. 37) argue that

> in earlier generations, it took a world war and a long time of conscious dismantling to get rid of the institutions that had evolved to support nationalism in the 1930s. Once these were stamped out, we saw an unprecedented march of a liberal world order. Unless existing elites understand the kinds of dynamics that underpin the rise of identity politics, they may see history repeat itself.

I do not completely share this pessimistic view of the future developments of populism within democracies. This book has demonstrated that populism works – or at least has so far worked – differently in established European democracies and in countries with younger democracies. Perilous nationalism in Western Europe in the 1930s emerged at a time when democracy in those countries was still young. Populists in power in developed economies today do not normally violate basic economic governance principles. However, some post-Brexit politicians, especially Donald Trump, have produced notable exceptions. We are about to see if these exceptions will grow into norms.

If even most populists have finally learned the economics lessons of the past, what can mainstream policymakers do further about the political environment in which populists flourish before they run out of time? In an environment of rapidly expanding social media influence on every aspect of our lives, it seems reasonable to embed a self-correcting mechanism in social media through carefully crafted regulation, which prevents mass voter manipulation. Leaving the most influential media of our time unregulated, and their sources of finance unexposed, means giving up on democracy. It also means serving up democracy's vital systems of checks and balances on a silver platter to the political entrepreneurs of the day.

Currently, the Western political and economic system seems unable to produce an effective response to the populist challenges of our time. Soon, we may look back on our time as the new dawn of mainstream populism. However, history has also demonstrated that populist waves are temporary. How long and how costly the current wave will be depends on our ability to learn from our past.

Bibliography

Alfaro, L., Kalemli-Ozcan, S., & Volosovych, V. (2008). Why doesn't capital flow from rich to poor countries? An empirical investigation. *The Review of Economics and Statistics, 90*(2), 347–368.

Auerbach, A. J., & Hassett, K. (2015). Capital taxation in the twenty-first century. *American Economic Review, 105*(5), 38–42.

Besley, T., & Persson, T. (2019). The rise of identity politics. Working Paper, London School of Economics.

Djankov, S., Montalvo, J. G., & Reynal-Querol, M. (2008). The curse of aid. *Journal of Economic Growth, 13*(3), 169–194.

Dornbusch, R., & Edwards, S. (1990). Macroeconomic populism. *Journal of Development Economics, 32*(2), 247–277.

Galston, W. A. (2018). The populist challenge to liberal democracy. *Journal of Democracy, 29*(2), 5–19.

Lucas, R. E. (1990). Why doesn't capital flow from rich to poor countries? *American Economic Review, 80*(2), 92–96.

Mankiw, N. G. (2015). Yes, $r > g$. So what? *American Economic Review, 105*(5), 43–47.

Piketty, T. (2015). Putting distribution back at the center of economics: Reflections on 'Capital in the twenty-first century'. *Journal of Economic Perspectives, 29*(1), 67–88.

Saez, E., & Zucman, G. (2019). Progressive wealth taxation. *Brookings Papers on Economic Activity* (Fall). Forthcoming.

Stankov, P., & Vasilev, A. (2019). Business reform outcomes: Why so different? *Journal of policy Modeling, 41*(6), 1109–1127.

Taggart, P., & Rovira Kaltwasser, C. (2016). Dealing with populists in government: Some comparative conclusions. *Democratization, 23*(2), 345–365.

Wessel, D. (2019). Who are the rich and how might we tax them more? Published online: October 15, 2019. Retrieved December 27, 2019 from https://www. brookings.edu/

Index

Taylor & Francis eBooks

www.taylorfrancis.com

A single destination for eBooks from Taylor & Francis
with increased functionality and an improved user
experience to meet the needs of our customers.

90,000+ eBooks of award-winning academic content in
Humanities, Social Science, Science, Technology, Engineering,
and Medical written by a global network of editors and authors.

TAYLOR & FRANCIS EBOOKS OFFERS:

A streamlined
experience for
our library
customers

A single point
of discovery
for all of our
eBook content

Improved
search and
discovery of
content at both
book and
chapter level

REQUEST A FREE TRIAL
support@taylorfrancis.com

Printed in the United States
by Baker & Taylor Publisher Services